Rain Dancing

Debra Jean Collett

DJCollett Publishing

Table of Contents

Preface: Sliding Glass Doors

I GUESS I should have been frightened when the thunder was so loud it made the sliding glass doors shake and vibrate. I got a rush of excitement, instead, as I anticipated the bright, penetrating flash of lightning that followed. It became a game to see if I could guess where the lightning was and how far away its strike would be.

I would often sit there all alone. It never seemed lonely, though. After all, I was watching nature's symphony, at its best. The contrast from the darkness of the night to the brightness of the lightning-sheeted sky made my eyes water, at times, but never stopped me from weathering the storm.

The glass doors seemed massive and heavy, yet when Mother Nature was performing, the doors became light and clear. I could see past the apple tree and was able to scan over the grass along the three-quarter-acre, back, lot to the row of iris and peony bushes. They were located at the end of my world. My world was fenced with large, fragrant, lilacs on the south; and irises on the west; and large, very climbable cherry trees on the north. In the front yards and yards of green grass encircled a large mound of rich, dark-brown soil. Small fragrant flowers spotted the mound, and the crowning glory—a massive boulder— majestically rested at its top.

Located in the long stretch of backyard was also a garden that was sheltered by two ancient Bing cherry trees. These two trees were spaced far enough apart for a handcrafted playhouse to nestle in between. That playhouse was built by my father with the same dedication and love as the house with the sliding glass doors. It was my retreat;

Rapunzel's castle, Genie's lamp, and Cinderella's ball all rolled up into one place, where I could become whomever I imagined.

As I sat watching the storm, the lightning reflected on the windows of the playhouse, and I recalled a big smile my dad wore on his face as he worked on it until it was completed. Of course, after completion an appropriate house warming was hosted by Mom and Dad, complete with decorations and refreshments.

Oh, the memories that flooded my mind while watching those storms! Once in a while I would be in a self-induced trance, only to be startled back to reality by the loud thunder. I raised my head to see the rain come pouring down. It made the sliding glass doors all a blur. Now I could no longer see the whole picture. My vision wasn't as clear as it was before the rain fell, and it seemed to cause considerable anxiety on my part. It changed everything. It interrupted my dreams and imagination. For just a few seconds I felt like I had lost control of my perfectly orchestrated life.

If I waited long enough, the storm would soon be over and my life could get back to normal. But wait! I didn't want the storm to be over. I looked forward to the thrill and escape it offered. The dreading of the storm came at first, but then after it was over, a certain disappointment followed. The storm brought thrilling opportunities to reflect, imagine, dream, and intensely explore the feelings I had deep inside about life and all the mysteries and miracles that come. I liked that about it.

So maybe watching the storm a little longer wasn't so bad. I pulled my knees to my chest, took a deep breath, and closed my eyes. I could hear the rain slipping away from the window and the thunder quieting. Things were dark, but peaceful. This storm, I thought, wasn't that scary. So I reserved myself a spot in front of the sliding glass doors for the next performance. Sleep easily came with the lullaby of rain falling faintly on the roof and the wonderfully clean smell it left behind. It was always a reminder to me that morning would bring a refreshed newness to my world.

Everyone would awake the next morning with individual accounts of the night's thunderstorm. Some would not even remember the storm or be affected by it. Others would relive it over and over because of the fear they might have experienced during its peak. And still others, including me, would reflect on the experience and tuck it away in a safe place of memory. Maybe it would come in handy someday, or maybe it might become my motivation to dance in the rain.

It took a lot of storms as I was growing up before I got the courage and acquired the knowledge to dance in the rain that is created by a storm. Obstacles kept holding me back. I was tired. It was dark. I didn't want to get cold. I used many excuses that I called reasons. Dancing in the rain comes naturally to some of us. We just do it. We follow our instincts and let go of inhibitions. Some of us need to be taught or coaxed. And there are some who have to do it as a challenge or a dare. No matter what the reason, if you learn or decide to dance in the rain, you will be able to feel pure joy. You will find that life will be better, more enjoyable, more positive, and more rewarding. You will feel the thrill and rush of the challenge and the rain will comfort any pain you might experience. The rain is a gift from God. It nourishes, strengthens, gives life, cleans and refreshes. Embrace it!

Storms always come in all sorts of sizes and forms. Some will be gentle and sneak up on you without warning. Some will be violent and hit you so hard that they cause damage. It may be the kind that you think cannot possibly be repaired. Storms will come that will leave such devastation and destruction that we will feel the very life of us being drawn into the storm's vacuum. Why then would anyone look forward to a storm? You might be thinking, "That's right! Do you think I am crazy to want suffering?" Not all storms are the kind you can sit by and watch peacefully through sliding glass doors. In real life, we all must face a storm. Some of us will have that opportunity more than others. I say *opportunity* because the storm is what gives us strength. As we weather a storm, we gain knowledge and understanding of many things that we need.

All of us at one point in our lives have heard the comparison of how a storm makes trees strong. You know the one I'm talking about?

The trees with the strongest root systems are usually the trees that have weathered winds and storms. They are stronger for it. The ones that have to stretch for sunlight become tall and straight, not bent over with the weight of adversity. This is very hard to do. And it is especially hard to do over and over. Some of us are required to do just that, repeat our efforts and prove ourselves again and again.

Just as we all have our storms, so do we all have our own sliding glass doors. They become the windows from which we view our world. They are the doors of opportunity. They offer us vision into the possibilities of life. There is no view that is restricted if we keep the glass clean and free of debris. We have choices to open our eyes and watch and learn or close them and listen and experience. Imagination and reflection can take place during a storm. The windows can offer some protection, but even they become clouded or blurred, which temporarily distorts our vision and we lose sight of the whole picture. At the time it seems like an eternal wait until the storm passes and our vision returns.

Of course, we also have the choice that so many make, and that is to avoid the storm at all costs. We can run away, try to hide, or retreat. Choices are always available. Some of us do not have a voice as to what kind of storm we must face or if we have to face a storm at all. But we all have a choice to decide how we are going to experience the storm. Don't be afraid to get a little wet. While you're waiting for the rainbow to come and the promise of hope for a better tomorrow, dig deep inside yourself. Find the motivation to dance in the rain. We all will do the dance differently, but the kind or method does not really matter. What matters is that we embrace the gifts that God has given us that we do not fear the storms, that we feel the cleansing power of the rain, and that we rejoice in all our unique possibilities.

As I reflect back on my life, I do remember the sliding glass doors in my parents' home vividly. I had a wonderful childhood with lots of great memories. I am average in many ways, and not so average in others. I want to tell about my experiences of storms and dancing in the rain. Mostly I want my children and grandchildren to understand

and feel things that our miraculous technical world will never be able to give. I want them to experience storms and dancing in the rain. If reading my story can give them motivation, or if it can help anyone who reads this, then I have again experienced the joy that is comparable to rain dancing.

We are all unique and valuable to our Father in Heaven. He has created the earth and all things in it for our good, enjoyment, and benefit. He loves us very much no matter what kind of storm we may face. He is always there for us, and after all, He did create the rain. We are the recipients of His love each and every day. He is our motivation, our teacher, and He provided us with His Son. Through having faith in our Savior and embracing the gifts we are given, we can and we will weather the storms of life. I pray that He will be with me as I tell my story and that I may portray the value of gratitude to Him who gave me the gift of life and who ultimately taught me how to dance in the rain.

Take Me Out to the Ballgame

WHAT'S MORE AMERICAN than baseball? Actually, baseball is thought of as an American standard. Most of us have memories of some sort of baseball influence in our lives; whether it was actually playing the game, watching or listening to the game, having friends or family members participate, or performing on the game stage ourselves. It isn't something that in this modern century is gender specific. The ballgame has produced heroes, challenged standards of fairness, evoked tempers, given new meaning to parental control, developed new and awkward vocabulary, and influenced millions of people.

For me, the game of baseball and other games that shared the same suffix were a staple and definitely a huge part of my growing up and adulthood. I wanted to be a ballplayer from the time I learned to walk, no pun intended, to the time I couldn't play but spent my time sitting on the sidelines. Later in my life, as I watched my children play and participate in various ballgames, I always felt as though I was there on the field. I took in every smell, sound, and sight. I stamped in my memory all that was said and done. It became a wonderful way to have instant replay on a personal basis.

My earliest recollection of the ballgame is connected with the person who taught me to value sports and the lessons they had to offer. That person was my father.

Dad always wore a baseball cap, except when he was at church. It was his recognizable trademark. He loved sports, especially baseball. When he was in high school he made the varsity baseball team as a sophomore. He was the team's pitcher. It was especially unique that Dad was their pitcher because he was left-handed. In fact he was the high school's first left-handed pitcher. One might not consider that fact so unusual or hard for someone. But until you have tried to teach a student or your child how to play ball, eat, write, sew, or anything that requires the use of their arms and hands and you are right-handed, you will never understand the seemingly innocent quirk that falls upon about a third of the population. Being left-handed adds unique challenges to life. But being unique in that respect made my father stand out from the crowd, and he became well known and very popular.

Dad was liked and respected by his peers. He was also admired by a special young lady, my mother. Mom recalled going to all of my dad's ballgames and even his practices. She was such a loyal fan! It seemed that her enthusiasm was a bit too much for the coach, though. He noticed her at the games and practices. He also noticed that my father did not pitch as well when he was distracted by my mother, so my mother was called into the coach's office one afternoon. The coach requested ever so strongly that she not attend my dad's games or practices from that time further. According to my mother, the coach stumbled over his words, trying to find the right way to tell her that if she wanted the school to win region or be able to go to the state tournament, she would stay away. She was told she was too much of a distraction for my dad.

The lecture didn't stop my mother. She still went to the games and practices. She just hid out of sight, where my dad couldn't see her, or at least she thought. And of course she never told him she was there. Dad told me later, when telling the story from his point of view that he always knew she was there and it really made him play better. Either way, the team went to state that year. My dad lettered all three years he was on the team. And thus began the American standard in my parents' lives.

My mother and father were married right after high school. It was popular to do at that time because of the outbreak of World War II. My mother often joked that Dad put the pressure on her to hurry and marry him. He said, "I am going off to war and we may never see each other again." (There's never been any drama in my family. No, not at all!). Anyway, Dad did join the Air Force to serve his country, they got married, which was a great blessing, and they started their lives together. Life by then would not be nearly as carefree as high school.

Apparently their beginnings were a little rocky. Mom tells the story that on their way to Salt Lake City to be married, she begged my dad, as she puts it, to turn around. She said she cried and told him that she wasn't ready to be married. He told her that she was and that he was not going to turn around because he loved her and wanted to be married. Mom finally stopped crying and having a panic attack. Dad told the story a little differently, involving not so many tears and certainly with no begging, just suggesting. In spite of the rocky beginning, my mother and father were able to make their lives and eventually their children's and grandchildren's lives full of lighthearted, humorous experiences and serious encounters that taught lessons and provided the peaceful joy that one receives when living life to the fullest.

Believe it or not, the ballgame of their lives took on more meaning than just rules, playing out the rules and the outcome. It sneaked in a flavorful influence of values, humor, integrity, perseverance, and friendship that was innately ingrained in their lives and eventually in mine.

Soon after they were married, they were transferred to Arizona. The Air Force had a military base there called Luke Field. My mother told me about various experiences they had while at Luke Field. They lived in a small, three-room apartment on the base that they shared with another couple. These wonderful people would later in their lives grow, along with their families, into old age together. It wasn't a coincidence that they would also share the love of the ballgame together too.

Sometimes in a ballgame a wise coach and team have backup plays readied and prepared. One time my parents' backup play nearly went sour. My father had been off base with my mother to see relatives and friends. Dad lost track of his time and panicked when he discovered he was late getting back on base. If he wasn't on time when he arrived on the base, the military would consider him AWOL, absent without leave, a serious offense in the military. But hey, my dad was a ballplayer, right? So his backup play went something like this: Mom would drive the Buick into the base with my dad securely tucked in the trunk of the car. That would be a cinch, or so they thought. When they arrived at the gate and the military police was about to wave them through, my mother stalled the car. She was so nervous she gave the throttle too much gas, and it flooded the engine. She fiddled with the starter and gas pedal several times as she worked up a sweat. My dad was in the trunk thinking he would be facing a court martial if my mother didn't get the car started and do it quickly. The MPs were about to stop the car and search it, under the hood and in the trunk as well, when the engine roared to a start, my mother sheepishly smiled and waved, and they went on their way. My parents laughed a lot about this experience later - much, much later. Mom and Dad danced in the rain a lot during their time at Luke Field. War time is a horrible storm by anyone's definition. But they remained positive, making the most of whatever they had and always remembering their sense of humor.

In the rules of baseball, you have several options when you get up to bat. You can swing three times to accomplish several things. You can hit a home run, which some consider the ultimate experience; you can bunt to just get on base; you can strategically try to place the ball where it won't get caught and thus getting you on base and perhaps a team member in to home; or you can get up to the plate, eye the pitcher down, and swing at the ball hard, doing the best you can do. And with doing the best you can do you have a surge of accomplishment and fulfillment of knowing you are a team player and you are needed for the success of the team and the advancement of the sport. The storms of baseball might be considered to be striking out, being tagged out as you slide into home, or having some show off catch the beautiful potential homerun that you just hit. Now that is a storm.

My parents would step up to the plate, figuratively speaking, many times in their lives. To be successful in any game, whether it is sports or life, you need to score points or meet your thought-out goals. Meeting those goals or making the points enables you to succeed. Success may not always be winning by being the team with the most points. It may be that you are the team that has learned the most valuable lessons or the one team that shows incredible sportsmanship and integrity. Win or lose, no matter the score, you must be willing to try at the game over and over in order to be able to eventually taste and feel success. One thing that coaches emphasize to team members is to keep trying until they succeed. They teach perseverance, to never give up.

My parents were well schooled in this particular area of life's lessons. They eagerly anticipated the birth of their first child, a boy. He was born on the base. It was late at night and an officer who was the acting physician on call attended my mother. There were one nurse and one assisting doctor there that night. My dad told me that he heard the baby cry out, which was a sign that things were stable and okay.

The physician that delivered my brother told my father and mother the baby had not taken a breath and there was nothing they could do. My father recalled the strong smell of alcohol on the doctor's breath as he related the terrible news. The baby was dead. There had not been any effort to revive him. From all appearances the baby looked healthy and fully formed. My parents had to insist on seeing him, and my mother wanted desperately to hold the infant. At first the doctors were not going to allow it, but my parents persevered and Mother and Dad lovingly held the beautiful ten-pound infant boy in their arms. He had large hands and lots of black hair, like Dad's. My father never dismissed the sounds of the baby's cry in the night, and my parents knew in their hearts that he had taken the breath of life. He was perfect. My parents took the baby back to Utah to give him a burial. They named him Kenneth James.

This was a devastating storm for my parents, the kind that did the damage that cannot be replaced or repaired. My parents were expecting the rainbow, the pot of gold, the reward that hard work brings, and the hope of success. Instead they faced a storm like no other—the loss of a child. The sweet joy a mother feels when she holds her newborn infant in her arms over and over again my mother would not feel. She would not have the remarkable experience of watching her infant grow into adulthood. The memories of labor and delivery would remain fresh in her mind because the infant, who would normally erase those painful memories, had left her side. He was gone. The storm hit hard and fast. It should have been prevented. Someone could have warned them. Surely this was possible, wasn't it?

The tiny plot where my brother was laid to rest was so small that it seemed lost among the other graves with their large, ornate headstones. I'm sure if one would have looked at this tiny parcel they wouldn't have been able to imagine the pure destruction and heartache from the storm that preceded it. They wouldn't have seen my mother's tear-stained face and sleepless expressions that adorned it. They wouldn't have been able to imagine the pain and torture she endured because of having a heart that was truly broken. How does one face or even imagine such a storm?

When I became a mother and held my children in my arms later in my life, I often would reflect on the experience that my mother and father had at Luke Field. Only then did I partially understand the magnitude of the event and the effect it had on their lives. I was not there. I wasn't watching them play out the ballgame close up or hiding in the background, but I have my mother's voice branded in memory, and I can clearly hear her telling and recalling every detail. I can see the disappointment in my father's face when he relived hearing the baby's cry and telling me how helpless and empty he felt. I wasn't there to see them get up to the plate to bat. I didn't see them swing hard over and over and try their best. But I have their wisdom and their vision in my mind and soul. The rules of the ballgame began long before I came to earth. I would definitely learn to be a team player thanks to my wonderful parents.

Not very many years passed before my mother became pregnant with my brother, Richard. He was born in my hometown and was delivered by a seasoned country doctor who was easy to trust and rely on, at least according to my mother. Richard didn't come into this world without incident, however. It was told by my mother that when he was born the doctor could not get him to breathe. They tried several state-of-the-art methods to induce spontaneous respirations and stimulate his heart, but nothing seemed to work. Then Doctor Merrill took a long hypodermic needle and shoved it through the middle of Richard's heart. It produced a response in the heart similar to the effect a defibrillator would have in more modern times. Mom and Dad definitely heard him scream and they cried, along with the doctor and the nurse, tears of pure undefiled joy. The baby weighed just over seven pounds and was bald and shiny as a brand new marble. With reddened face and piercing screams my brother entered life reluctantly. My parents didn't seem to mind and immediately and willingly overlooked my brother's flaws and shortcomings. They would always do just that.

Richard grew up with two parents who adored and loved him greatly. My dad gave my mother some money one Mother's Day to purchase for herself a much-needed dress. My mother then used that money to purchase a red toy fire truck for Richard rather than spend the money on herself. This was so typical of my mother. This was only one of thousands of sacrifices my mother made for her children and later her grandchildren. She was always a great team player and exemplified the concept of teamwork. Her actions often produced better team results rather than individual glory.

My parents were extraordinary at teaching unconditional love. They taught us a lot about the connection between sacrifice and charity, the true love of Christ. To be able to put someone else's needs above your own is a priceless character trait to have and is rare to see in anyone. Because God understood man's weaknesses and his tendency to be self-centered, He wisely worded the second commandment, "Love thy neighbor as thyself." It is when we finally and willingly forget ourselves and think of the needs of others that we truly become team players. Selflessness is the character building block of a winning team, whether it is the team of life or the family or literally a sports team. There are lots of teams that we are a part of and there are continuous ballgames to play.

Richard became my dad's greatest sports fan. Dad taught my brother to play ball almost before he could walk. He was throwing balls of all kinds at a very young age. Mom and Dad were enjoying every minute of every hour of his life. I know, because of the reflections of memory they lovingly told me and also because of the hours we spent as a family watching home movies. The home movies back in the 1950s weren't as perfected as they are now. They were black and white with no sound. Eventually they were modernized to include sound and color. I affectionately look back on the black-and-white no-sound movies for this reason: Mom and Dad loved to narrate every detail and would often include appropriate voice fluctuation to match the person on the screen. In my brother's case, their voices portrayed immense pride and deep joy when they spoke about him.

My parents took Richard everywhere with them, and they did everything together.

This was the making of an ideal team. They were scoring and constantly improving their game plans. One of those plans was my father's. He was close to getting his commercial pilot's license, but had to decrease his actual flight time when my brother was born. He spent more time working and providing than he did flying. However, my parents became resourceful and creative in order to accomplish this very important goal of my father's. When my brother was nearly a year old, my parents flew a small aircraft to the Detroit area to pick up a new car. The flight distance was long enough that it would put my dad well within range of logging enough flight hours to get his license. Most people would have left a young child home with a baby sitter and relished the time they could spend alone with each other, but not my parents. Richard went right alongside them as he would do for the rest of his life on this earth. He later in life would be separated by distance at times, but he would always be in their hearts and by their sides forever.

The team approach to the ballgame of life was present from the beginning of our family. The three of them made a great team. I came along, eventually, and I really didn't disturb that harmony at all. I was welcomed with as much enthusiasm and love as my brother. I quickly became Daddy's little girl and Mother's pride. I was spoiled with love and attention from the start. I remember the movies we watched throughout our childhood, and particularly I remember pictures of my brother trying hard to hold me as a baby and not let me slide off of his lap. His grin was big as he held me. He must have made a secret promise to himself and to who knows who else to protect me and to magnify the calling of "big brother." Richard became my hero as I grew up. I remember the love I saw in his eyes as I watched the home movies graduate from holding me as a baby, helping me walk, and then walking by my side to church in our new, best Easter outfits. Our team certainly had character. That point was unmistakable. It showed through the smiles and the body language of the dozens of life experiences caught on film.

Now I was old enough to remember things on my own. The memories I have of the ballgames are what I experienced firsthand, not what I was told. And one of the earliest I recall goes something like this: My brother began playing Little League baseball as soon as he could carry a bat. He wasn't quite old enough to play, but my dad was the coach, and the assistant coach had no objections to my brother playing, probably because my brother was an extraordinary ball player. Primed from childhood to be a star, Richard was now up to bat, so to speak. It was the bottom of the seventh inning with loaded bases. (In baseball language this is intense!) The scenario was set and the game continued.

We had a swing set in our backyard. Richard used to pump himself higher and higher and then lunge forward, catapulting himself out of the swing like a runner approaching a broad jump.

He would land on both feet for the most part, losing his balance only on occasion. He would then quickly climb back in the swing and repeat the process, trying to reach a mark farther away than the previous one.

One time—and it only took one—he landed with his legs straight. He forgot to bend his knees. The result was painful and he was urgently taken to the doctor. Dr. Merrill, the physician who had delivered Richard, discovered that upon landing with straight legs and with the speed and force placed on his legs, Richard had forced the head of his left femur up into his hip joint, which caused considerable pain and made the left leg shorter than the right. After adjusting the leg position while my brother was under anesthetic, the doctor carefully placed a metal brace on Richard's leg. It had two metal bars that ran the length of the entire side of his leg. It was very heavy, and it did not bend. Later he was fitted with a special shoe for his left leg. The shoe had a raised sole, which made his right leg even with his left. He walked straight legged and with a limp. Running was out of the question. He was to remain like this for up to a year.

The ballgames literally came to an end for my brother, at least temporarily. He tried to run, but just could not make it happen. The storm came. He watched his friends continue to play baseball in Little League, ride their bikes, run, and play as young boys normally do. He took his share of teasing and ridicule. Those who were jealous of his talents in baseball before were now openly celebrating his absence from the team. My father watched, wanting it to be himself to suffer, not his son. Mother cried as she silently asked God if she had done something wrong to have her son suffer in such a cruel way.

Many fathers and mothers must stand by and watch their children suffer in pain and agony. A flood of emotions fills their hearts and pierces their souls. I have felt those emotions as a parent. If we have children or influence them in some way, we feel this kind of emotion when they hurt or suffer. Often as caregivers or relatives, as teachers or friends, we are required to witness a variety of suffering and trials. Unfortunately children are not exempt from these storms of life.

They are in the ballgame, like it or not. We, their parents, chose life for them. We cannot control the outcome; we can only influence it.

So it is with our Father in Heaven. He chose life for His son. His son volunteered to enter that life with a selfless mission, to be our Savior. Our Father watched His son grow from infancy to manhood, and not without storms. He felt the agony that a parent feels when a child is in need and as a parent you cannot or should not help. Sometimes they need to do it on their own. They have to face some storms alone to gain their strength. It fulfills a purpose that is essential to our existence and our eternal wellbeing. Our Father and our Elder Brother knew this in the preexistence. We knew we were to come to earth to receive a body and be tested. We knew we were to be a part of a team, and we also knew we would have storms to face. But after these storms we were also given hope and a promise of a better tomorrow. It is up to us to teach our children and their children to face the storm with faith, not fear, and to learn to dance in the rain.

My parents accomplished that with my brother. Dad kept throwing the ball with him the entire time he was being treated for his injury. He taught him how to be the best pitcher that the Little League Baseball Association would ever see. And as an added bonus, lugging that heavy brace on his leg strengthened his muscles and made him stronger, so that eventually he would be a faster runner than most kids his age.

Soon the storm began to end and the ballgame resumed. The day my brother got his brace off, my dad took him out to a river a short distance from our house. It was called the Bear River. It was small compared to most, but it was deep enough to harbor the brace, which my brother picked up and tossed as hard as he could into the river. He jumped up and down and screamed with excitement. He cried tears of happiness and embraced my father with the pure love that a father and son feel for each other. They both felt the satisfaction of weathering a violent storm. They had danced in the rain.

Richard now had another chance to be up to bat in the ballgame. And I do believe he set his sights high. He wanted a homerun so badly it became his motivation to be able to keep dancing in the rain, to be the team player, and to weather the storm. It became the short future goal that was set for himself to achieve and that would enable him to feel the pride of accomplishment.

My dad took my brother's Little League team that year to the World Series of Little League Baseball. They made it far enough in the playoffs that they played for the championship. This accomplishment was a fulfillment of both of their dreams.

The whole town helped with the preparation and the arrangements. The team members and their mothers had bake sales, and the newspaper even featured an article about the team and its bold endeavor. There was a small, printed message at the end of the article. It directed anyone who wanted to contribute a donation to the team to do so at the local bank where an account had been set up for them by the mayor. The excitement grew and eventually involved the news media. The story was followed by the TV news as a character feature in their nightly broadcast.

I was only six years old when these events took place. I couldn't read the papers, but I listened to the television programs with my family, and I was the privileged sibling of the year! I was the official back-up batgirl for the team. Of course most of the time I spent in the dugout sitting on the bench while watching my dad and brother at play. But every now and then my dad would send me out to home plate to fetch the discarded bat that was covered in dust and return it to the holes in the chain-linked fence. These holes magically encased the bat handle and dangled the rest of the bat safely until it was needed again. I usually required some assistance from the regular batboy and my father when I retrieved the massive hitting tools, for the bats were heavy and almost as tall as me. I became a fast runner like my brother. It was a skill I acquired out of necessity.

Each time I pinpointed my destination, marked in my mind the occupancy of third base, and then ran like crazy to home plate. My heart raced, which provided the adrenaline my short little legs needed to fetch the bat and return to the dugout before the next player was up to bat or to avoid a surprise runner from sliding into home. My biggest fear was I would be stuck at home plate and in the way of that sliding runner from third base. Thanks to my dad, it never happened. He was always there to rescue me from any potential harm or danger. It would be that way my whole entire life.

The time soon arrived for the big game. The family was fortunate that the series was held in Toole, Utah, that year, which made it easier and affordable for all the families to attend and see their team players become childhood heroes. Toole was about a four-hour drive from our home. At that point in time there had not been any interstate highways built. In fact the interstate concept was barely becoming an idea, so the journey was made in a 1958 Buick on a long, boring, highway with only two lanes, one coming and one going. It was un-usually scary for a six-year-old.

As we drove into town that morning, I sensed the excitement of the event. There were crowds of people of all ages, families with small children, and the designated baseball hero walking by his father's side. He was fully clothed in the uniform of his team, complete with matching cap and socks. His shirt was tucked neatly inside his knee-length baseball pants and there was a glove on one hand. The other hand threw and precisely snapped a baseball into the glove as they walked. The father walked straight up and proudly placed his hand on his son's shoulder. He too wore the cap of his little hero's team. Norman Rockwell would have basked in the scenes found there that day. Who knows? Perhaps he did.

It was a three-day tournament, and we went directly to the home of the host family. They generously gave us room and board for three nights. I don't remember too much about them. I do remember, how-ever, that they had a girl about the same age as my brother, and she started to go gaga over my brother as soon as we started up their porch steps. I laughed at him and rolled my eyes as he turned a bright pinkish red. He turned his face away so no one would see his lips but me and mouthed, "Shut up!"

The ballgames were intense. I was not allowed to be batgirl

because of the tournament rules. The boys on the team made a huge fuss over me and always made me feel like I was such an important part of the team. I really believed I was just that, essentially irreplaceable. Extra players had earned the privilege to come to the series. Not every boy got to play each inning. My father tried to be fair to all the boys. After all, this was an opportunity of a lifetime, and many of them would never get the experience for themselves again and would more than likely not even get it with their own sons later in their lives. It was really a big deal!

I was used to being around the team, in the dugout, taking the players drinks of water and being part of the guys. I went through abrupt withdrawal at the tournament series. I would wait for my mother to be totally absorbed in the game, especially when my brother was pitching, and then I would make my move. Slowly I sneaked away and found myself at the dugout. My small fingers clawed the chain link fence as I pressed my face and nose up against it. Occasionally I released my stronghold on the fence and jumped up and down to see over the heads of the boys in the dugout. They were always standing up. Loud cheers and hollering deafened my tender ears. I wasn't having much fun anymore.

One of the boys who had been sitting on the bench turned around to talk to me. "Hey, if I give you a quarter, would you go get me some Bit-a-Honey? I'll let you have a piece." I was relieved to have something to do, so I eagerly nodded my head, grabbed the quarter, and a few minutes later returned with the stash. The small pieces of candy were soft and warm and some stuck to the paper wrapper because the day was extremely hot. It seemed like I had just begun to savor the flavor and genuine treat of the morsels when the boys yelling and cheering pierced my ears. We had won!

After running their victory sweep around the bases, the team helped pick up the equipment. Dad was busy talking to parents and giving congratulations to the assistant coach, which was immediately returned with vigor. Suddenly I felt two hands under my arms and I was swiftly swept up in the air and firmly placed on the shoulders of

Bill. Bill was my Bit-a-Honey buddy. He was unusually tall for his age and pencil skinny. I thought all the boys were big and strong, and from a six-year-old viewpoint, they all towered way up there. Bill was kind to me. He was only twelve years old, but he showed the sensitivity and maturity of someone much older. Later in his life he would eventually become a pediatrician and the kindest doctor our small town would know.

The award ceremony was crowded and lots of cameras were flashing. My brother and my father ventured out to the pitcher's mound to receive a special trophy for the team and an individual one for my brother. Richard always excelled in everything he did. He made the news, along with the team and the coaches. But it was the picture of my brother receiving his trophy and shaking the hand of the president of the Little League Association that caught everyone's attention that day and forever. The boy who had been in a brace for a year, who was told he might never play ball again, and who was much younger than the rest of his team, had produced his own special miracle. He not only played ball and did it very well, he danced and danced in the rain, and then, he danced some more.

That storm became a whisper of wind and a spray of mist in our memories. Often when a storm has ended, we can close our eyes and slowly take in a deep breath. We feel the freshness of the rain and smell the clean, tempting air. It almost always brings a smile. When I think of these wonderful times in my childhood, I feel the freshness and smell the effects of the lasting memories. I hear the cheers of the crowds. I see the bright lights in the stadium. I watch in my mind's eye the wonderful experiences unfold year after year as I grew up and played softball, as I learned to pitch from my father and as I eventually coached several of my own teams to championships. I can still hear the crack of the bat as it hits the ball, and I feel the smooth softness of the leather mitt. I still sense the excitement and anticipation of the whole experience. The sounds engulf me. I embrace the smells and sights. I note the lessons learned and taught. And still to this day, I will never be too old to ask, "Can you take me out to the ballgame?"

Try It Risk Free!

OH, HOW WE are tempted and lured into trying products, events, skills, experiences, objects, and yes, even life. A constant barrage of choices is placed before us daily, and often our choices are scrutinized and judged by the people who surround us. Even as we enter this world, we are strongly encouraged to breathe, and we are scored immediately on our collective efforts. It is called an Apgar score and is the medical test we are given as soon as we make our first appearance. We are judged immediately, almost before we have a chance to protest or have a say in what is happening. The results of this first, small test bring a sigh of relief or a serious cause for concern to our welcoming committee. Either way, trying life as we know it is not risk free.

In the preexistence our loving Father explained, I'm sure, about the body we would receive, the life we would live on earth and the tests we would face. I feel because He loved us so deeply that He made sure we understood that our lives would not be without risks and possible failures. But He wanted desperately for us to succeed and return to Him. Therefore, He provided the means, guidance, and tools necessary to accomplish a successful reunion. We were not lured into an empty endeavor that would benefit only the one proposing it. Contrarily, we were given a most precious gift: agency. We freely and willingly chose to participate in our Father's Plan of Happiness. And for extra insurance, we would have our Older Brother's atoning sacrifice to ensure our readiness for the journey and give us the opportunity to exemplify faith. I'm sure our contractual agreement included a spiritual money-back guarantee, so to speak. We would be given and rewarded the treasures of Heaven just for giving life a try. We were promised blessings unmeasured, ones that were beyond our comprehension.

After hearing the proposals and what was offered, two-thirds of our Father's children made a clear and informed decision to willingly come to earth for this trial, a trial in living life with all the risks and with no guarantee of smooth sailing or the absence of storms. You and I were willing to take any risks to be here because of those promises made in the contract between our Father in Heaven and us. Those promises were to receive a body of flesh and blood that would conquer death because of Jesus Christ, to be resurrected in time with a reuniting of body and spirit and eternal life and progression. This promise was conditioned on keeping our contract to obey His commandments and worship only Him during our trial on earth.

In the real world, risk-free trials are an illusion, whether they are spiritual, emotional, or temporal ones. You risk side effects from products tried, injuries from faulty or malfunctioning equipment, and sometimes damage to body and soul. The list goes on and on. The concept of risk-free living with guaranteed happiness without effort is a concept that seeps from the dark influence of the Evil One, Satan. I have an awakening awareness of the risks involved in living and the anticipation of taking chances on a daily basis. Think about it; so do all of us. And we are all blessed with agency and can choose to make decisions every day. How we face those challenges and weather our personal storms determines the degree of joy we experience here on earth. It's what we make of those choices that truly define any perceived risks. We are in this trial of life together. All of us are interconnected and have much more in common than we think. So here is what I have to say about life, "Try it! You'll like it!" I know I did. This is how it began. Like Nephi, I was born of goodly parents.

The circumstances and environment that we are born into definitely play a major role in how our life experiences unfold. And so it has been with me. I was extremely blessed and fortunate to be born into a home where the gospel of Jesus Christ was taught and the example of unconditional love was prominent. My family was not wealthy, monetarily, but rich with heritage and traditions. I learned the distinction, early in my life, between wants and needs. My parents were resourceful, creative, and fugal. They tried to pass that wisdom onto their children.

Mom and Dad had grown up during the Depression. They learned through that violent storm of life how to have true gratitude and appreciation for small things and show wonder toward the world that so many of us take for granted. The concept of saving to acquire a want or a need was a given rule followed diligently. Taking care of each other and repairing your belongings were deeply engrained in both of my parents. Also they could multitask masterfully. Developing talents was a given responsibility in life, according to their wisdom, and my siblings and I were taught to revere God and show gratitude to Him for our life. My parents taught with mesmerizing example to serve others and make life good for ourselves, neighbors, and family. Our tools and resources to accomplish these ever-so-important goals came to us by using the talents and skills that God had given us.

Dad was considered a jack of all trades. He could fix absolutely everything. Many of his skills were self-taught and served him extremely well. His skills and unique talents were useful and eventually became a legacy that was crafted by love and hard work. Dad showed promise in certain fields—carpentry, electrical, plumbing, and mechanical. Oh, and I need to mention he was a mailman and salesman by profession. Everything else that didn't fall under these categories, he did in his spare time!

He enjoyed sports, especially baseball. He played a variety of sports long into his marriage. With the invention of the television, Dad loved to watch all of his favorite events, giving particular attention to boxing which Mom hated. She once said, "I think if I died while a ballgame was on, your dad would have them put me on ice until it was over."

Dad loved to hunt, fish, camp, and experiment with adventure, never flinching or hesitating to try something new. He valued hard work, gleaned joy from activity, and honored the beauty of the world around him. His living left a remarkable legacy.

Mom was equally as talented. She cooked savory meals that were complete with homemade bread, rolls, and frozen strawberry jam. Mom didn't have much patience for sewing with a machine, only to use it for mending. But later in life she proved her lack of patience theory wrong when she taught herself how to needlepoint and petit point. This type of needlework is meticulously and laboriously detailed. Mom was a true artist in every way. She loved the creations of our world, and she brought them home by using flowers. Hours were spent arranging bouquets for Memorial Day, and our home was always adorned with gorgeous, expensive-looking vases of flowers, which were changed seasonally as she saw fit. Mom was resourceful by canning fruits and vegetables, planting a garden, and attending diligently to the myriad of fruit trees on our property. She kept an immaculately clean home, and one of her favorite statements was, "At least when I die they can put on my headstone, She Kept a Clean House." My mother served as a teacher, nurse, chauffer, counselor, coach, and professional storyteller. When she wasn't occupied with all these marvelous talents, she worked at a local bank as a part-time teller.

Even though my parents had all of these outstanding accomplishments, the time they devoted to these talents did not for one instance shadow their most important talent and responsibility–that of mother and father. It was their most cherished calling.

My parents acquired a large parcel of land in the town where I was born. Their plan was to build a dream home, eventually, on part of it. Like their method of teaching their children, the method they used to accomplish this dream was the same—line by line, a little at a time. They began to save, plan, and live life. Dad built their first home. This starter home is where Kenneth had his funeral, Richard received the new red fire truck, and the twins came into their lives. It was also the home where I made my debut. It was a small, modest, rambler-style home and certainly did not extend to the borders of the entire parcel. Mom insisted on having large windows in front and a porch that extended the entire length of the front part of the house. It had grey wooden siding with green trim that surrounded the window and door frames. A garage sat distinctly to the south with a small walkway dividing it from the main house.

The world in the rear of our home was sectioned into partitions, starting with grass. It then continued with a garden area and then an area where an isolated miniature barn sat. A small calf was its tenant. I recall a few years later, after the calf grew and became a milk cow, trudging through the snow to the little barn to milk the cow with my dad. The snow was so deep that I could barely see over it, and I struggled to lift my little legs high enough to make the next step. Dad would use his oversized waterproof waders to make canyon-sized footprints for me. He held my hand and instructed me to step into the footprint and follow him. This simple scenario of a child trusting and following a loving father paints in my mind's eye another picture of a Father making footprints for us to follow, taking our hand, and guiding us in a similar way. My Heavenly Father has taken my hand and provided a way for me to overcome the seemingly insurmountable walls of cold, icy snow in my life.

Dad was a mail carrier for the postal service, and he worked a night job at a local store bagging groceries to meet the needs of his young family. Richard was a small child about four or five years old. Mother was expecting the twins. This house had harbored many sad memories and experiences and still they eagerly anticipated the future with hope and excitement. One of the miracles of modern science, and one that we take for granted, is ultrasound. Doctors and patients didn't have the blessing of ultrasound back then, and many couples didn't find out the gender of their babies until they were born. This was the case with the twins. No one knew the gender of the infants, nor did they have the miracle of seeing them on film or screen before their actual birth, a luxury afforded to this modern generation. Mom knew that she was carrying twins only because Dr. Merrill had found two heartbeats. That gentle country doctor did not have the convenience or security of the technology we know today. He used his God-given talents and gifts. He loved his profession.

Again, my parents were ecstatic with anticipation of another birth of a child. This excitement seemed to blot out the sad and painful memories of their firstborn's death. Any mother or father realizes very soon that there are incredible risks involved with the conception and birth of a child. My parents were keenly aware of the possible complications this particular pregnancy could bring, and it did. This bittersweet trial would prove to be morbidly intense and test their faith. It would shake and attempt to compromise the foundation of values that they had firmly set as building blocks in their lives.

When Mom was about five months into her pregnancy, she felt a significant decrease in activity. A cold-steel panic overwhelmed her. She urgently went to see Dr. Merrill only to have her hopes shattered with more devastating news. One heartbeat only could be found after an hour of careful searching, which led to the conclusion that one of the twins had died in the womb. Mom went into premature labor. It was much too soon for the other, vital twin to be born, and it was expected that the baby would not survive.

Miracles surround us everywhere. An event that was unheard of at that time took place that day. The twin that died in the womb was born and pronounced dead. She was a beautiful, fully formed, dainty little girl. To my mother's horror, the hospital disposed of the baby's body, and it was cremated. Mom never held her, only briefly glanced at her as the tiny infant's body was whisked away. Kaylene, as she was called by my parents, did not receive a burial. Her precious spirit directly returned to Father in Heaven. She, like Kenneth, was perfect. Her single mission and trial was to receive a body just like her brother. Knowing that they would see her again and hold her comforted my parents, but her cremation would torment my mother for the rest of her life. She had felt her child's life, though brief. Her presence was a part of my mother, as only a mother knows. The bond was there and very real. Not taking the breath of life did not minimize this truth. Her body would be resurrected and united with her spirit again, and joyful reunions would commence. Mother knew this to be true.

The miracle that took place that day was notable in the medical books. The other twin was born early, but healthy. Her life was spared. She had a chance at survival and screamed her arrival and approval of the opportunity. Doctor Merrill noted this miracle in his medical journal. Kaylyn entered this life with vigor and fight. She weighed only a little over four pounds. Mom and infant stayed in the hospital for weeks. Dad and his inquisitive five-year-old made daily trips to the hospital. Richard needed constant reassurance that Mom would actually come back home.

Finally the day arrived when Mom and Dad could take their miracle baby home. She was tiny and fragile, but her spirit was strong and determined. Dad told me later that Kaylyn was a very stubborn baby and knew exactly what she wanted. At night she had trouble sleeping, like most newborns. Dad slept with the baby's bassinet placed close to the bed and up toward the head, just so he could reach inside the bassinet and gently cradle her head in the palm of his hand, and then she would sleep. He tells that sometimes he slept for four or five hours at a time in that position. Mom told me later in my life that every time Dad would move, even a little, Kaylyn would wake up screaming. She certainly made her presence in this life known, and her influence was strong and effective, even though she was just a tiny infant.

The worry and sleepless nights prevailed for some four months. Then unexpectedly, Kaylyn became desperately ill. She was hospitalized and put in an iron lung. The mechanical breathing machine aided her respiratory efforts. She had pneumonia, and breathing was difficult. My parents and the nurse attended her around the clock, taking turns feeding her. Doctor Merrill was by her side using his medical expertise and evoking blessings from God. Kaylyn was removed from the breathing machine only for feedings. There was not much time to hold and comfort her. Everyone watched with wrenching heartache as her life slipped slowly and quietly away. Her sweet, beautiful spirit returned to her Heavenly home.

Kaylyn came into this life knowing the risks that it would bring. She fought valiantly with the aid of the talents she brought with her, stubbornness and perseverance.

Within forty-eight hours from the onset of her illness, she slipped quietly from this life and joined her brother and sister; perfect, unblemished spirits. The risks had been taken and my parents would not have done anything differently, for they cherished every detail of her short life. These memories helped to sustain my parents throughout their mortal lives. The experience became the driving force of their unwavering faith. This, too, became a devastating storm that had not reached the calm.

The heartache intensified for both of them as they buried their second child in another tiny grave. It was next to Kenneth's. Going through a funeral at their home again and losing a third child to death was almost unimaginable for anyone to comprehend. This kind of event evokes questions, tears, shock, and even anger.

For my mother, the tears never stopped. Every time she brought back to memory the vivid day-to-day existence of my sister, her eyes swelled with tears and she could hardly take a breath. In her wisdom, though, she taught me some valuable lessons about this experience. I would ask simple questions when I was young and more complicated, deep ones later. There was always one that remained the same. "How come you are not angry at God, Mom?"

My soft, gentle mother would take me in her arms and ask a question right back. "And what good would that do? It wouldn't bring her back, and it would make me very unhappy. Angry people cannot be happy people." She taught me by her unwavering faith in God and her knowledge of the truth that He answers prayers, always. Our prayers may not be answered immediately or exactly how we would like, but they are answered. Sometimes I listened in shock and amazement at her wise explanations and recognized the unwavering confidence she had in her beliefs.

Both my parents went through mourning for their daughter. Part of the grieving process includes some form of anger. That is very normal.

She was angry at first, but I was surprised to find out that it wasn't at God, it was at herself. Mom felt that she was not meant to be a mother; that she had done something wrong and somehow was being punished.

Later Mom taught me one of the most valuable lessons I have learned in my life. It goes like this: "God does not punish his children with tragedy. He loves each of us, individually and completely." Mom explained to me how she received the answer to her prayer. She was vacuuming one afternoon, and a peaceful feeling completely filled her and overcame her mind. She felt and knew in her heart, then and thereafter, that the babies were not taken from her because she was evil or not a good mother, but rather just the opposite. She had the knowledge revealed to her mind that she had done some very righteous things in the preexistence, thus was rewarded with three perfect spirits, spirits that needed to come to earth only to get a body and then would return to Father in Heaven. Their presence with Him was assured in the celestial kingdom of God. What more of an honor could be bestowed on my wonderful mother than to have the privilege of giving life to three of God's children who would be celestialized? The promise of the resurrection would later fill her empty arms and heart and she would see her babies again. This she knew. This she taught. This she lived.

I think most people, including myself, would have stopped trying to increase their family at that point. My parents certainly had embraced the challenges, risks, and trials. Emotionally they had taken a beating. It would have been understandable to "cut their losses" and make do with what they had. My parents were persevering with unshakable faith. They forged ahead clinging to the faint, unexplainable recollection of the bonds they felt to the preexistence and the truths that enabled them to look to the future.

A year later, I entered the family here on earth. I was told that I looked just like my sister Kaylyn. I can't imagine how hard that must have been for my mother. But Mom said she was elated and adored me. Of course I was not as stubborn as my sister, and Dad didn't have to sleep with his hand under my head, but nevertheless, I had my own demands and quirks. For some months after my birth, my parents both spent several sleepless nights as they would awaken to check on me just to make sure I was still breathing. Richard had been through a funeral and burial of a sibling just a year earlier, and he was young, so it was understandable how he clung to me, constantly adorning my forehead and cheeks with six-year-old kisses. Instantly he became my protector and admirer.

I cannot recollect my infancy and can rely only on the stories I have been told and the yards and yards of film that was shown religiously in our home. It became a main event. Home movies were experienced with the family, Uncle Dean, and Iva Beth and completed with homemade ice cream from the freezer.

Dad had an unusual relationship with my uncle, Dean. Dean was my mom's younger brother. Our families were close, literally. My uncle built their first home next to my parents' dream home. Dad and Dean even went into business ventures together. They acted more like brothers than brothers-in-law. Dean helped Dad in building their homes, running a business, and fixing cars and completely relished tormenting his nephew and niece. The truth is Dean loved us as he loved his own children.

Dean also loved Coca-Cola. I remember pictures of Dean in his high-water Levi's, white socks, penny loafers, and white crew-neck T-shirt. He wore his hair short and cropped and made stationary with styling gel known as Dippity-Do. A classic bottle of Coca-Cola was found in one hand or the other. Dean had an infectious smile and was carrying a confident air about him most of the time.

These happy times of my early infancy and toddlerhood brought pure joy into the hearts of my parents and extended family. Mom's family was very close. Living on the ranch and growing up with only her siblings for companionship and playmates made it that way for her. Later they all remained close to each other, and we benefitted as their children. Rich, valuable memories were formed and shaped several generations of my family. Mom's brothers and sisters had felt the sting and heartache of my parents' losses, so when I was born everyone celebrated and I seemed to have the undivided attention of my immediate and extended family. My uncles really doted on me and spoiled me.

I was barely walking in the first of many events that were caught on film. One in particular involved Dean and his signature cola bottle. I was trying awkwardly to toddle across the grass toward something that had caught my attention and was luring me to walk forward with my hands and arms extended, as if at any given moment I would grasp the prize I sought. Then I finally reached my hard-earned destination. A bottle of Coca-Cola was held by my uncle and strategically tipped at a perfect angle to give me the ability to slurp a taste, followed by a shiver and grimacing facial expression. But then like most young toddlers, I turned and opened my mouth like a little bird, anticipating more. My uncle gave me several drinks of cola from his bottle. And I liked it! My family teases me still that I started my cola addiction before I could walk. This became a family joke and subject of teasing for me for the rest of my life. I would never live it down.

When I was about four years old we moved from that first home to an apartment a few blocks away. Dad, Dean, and Dad's half-brother, Jay, started working on another home.

It was located by the creek. My brother, Richard, and I helped Dad and Mom clear the yard for planting grass. The yard had previously been an old river bed, so you can imagine how many large round rocks we hauled to the creek. Load after load was carefully dumped from Dad's old, green wheel barrel. I could barely pick up the rocks, and I didn't really do much to help, but my father smiled at me in a way that gave me the feeling that I was needed. His large grin and expression told me that he enjoyed watching my efforts and participation. I was a platinum blond six-year-old who wore my hair in braids and enjoyed being a tomboy, especially if it meant working alongside my dad. As a reward for hauling the rocks to the creek, Dad promised to unload a pile of sand in the front of the yard just for me. At least I thought it was just for me. Richard thought it was just for him.

That sand pile came soon, and I spent hours in it. One afternoon some older boys were walking in the middle of the road and purposefully detoured to the sand pile to taunt and tease me. They roughly scuffed the sand with their shoes, and it blew in my face, getting in my eyes. I immediately ran to the house with tears running down my face. The tears were from the sand irritating my eyes, not because the little creeps threw sand at me.

Mom was watching from the large, picture window awaiting the possibility of having to do damage control and give hugs with empathy as mothers do for an injured child. But I didn't go in the house as my mom expected. She was prepared to soften the hurt and dry the tears, but to her surprise, I bypassed the front door, went to the garage, retrieved a handle from a broken rake, and then, carrying the pole that was bigger than me, I chased after the boys with vengeful determination. I could barely carry the pole.

Mom came after me, explaining that I shouldn't go after those boys to hurt them. I never could understand until later why she had a hard time telling me and not laughing. I was very independent and determined to take care of things myself. The self-preservation instinct that I developed as a young child would prove extremely useful in my future. Anyway, the boys seemed scared. At least, they ran pretty fast.

I worshipped my older brother and wanted to be just like him. I liked to climb trees, play ball, and throw rocks in the creek. Dad always included me in fishing and hunting excursions. Never was I excluded because I was a girl. In fact, for much of my young life my dad had me convinced that he needed me to go pheasant hunting with him. In my mind, I was the reason he did so well at the hunt. Dad smiled proudly at my innocence of believing him when he told me that I had better vision than anyone, and I could spot the birds before he could. I soon realized that Dad just painted that illusion to make me feel special and that the time he spent with his daughter was as important to him as the time he spent with his son. He had a special way of showing that fact often.

It became Mom's challenge to develop my femininity. Shirley

Temple was a popular child actress at that time. She was unique, and the whole world was in love with the little star. My mom was no exception. Mom enrolled me in tap, ballet, and tumbling classes. I even learned the hula, complete with grass skirt. My childhood became a collage of costumes, rehearsals, makeup, and daunting music to tap to, "On the Good Ship Lollipop," for example. I even had to have my hair cut short and permed into soft curls that framed my face like the child actress. I was okay with the short haircut, as I was as much a tomboy as I was a Shirley Temple wannabe.

I recall crying hard and long after one haircutting session because the stylist did not give me a "butch" haircut. A butch was a razor-to-head buzz cut. The only part I hated about getting my hair cut was the way it made me itch and sneeze. The stylist and Mom were constantly telling me to hold still. I tried hard. I wrinkled my nose over and over for relief. I crossed my feet and tapped my fingers under the gigantic, plastic coverup that was designed for an adult and to catch an adult amount of cut hair. But my efforts were to no avail. I would return from my appointment each time with red, swollen eyes, running nose, and sneezing bouts. We finally, after years, discovered that I was allergic to my own hair. The cut made me miserable and the permanents were stinky, burned my eyes, and took forever. I was tortured into being a feminine little girl.

Mom experimented by letting me grow my hair longer, so it didn't have to be cut as often, thinking that would solve the problem of allergies. But then I would cry and wiggle as Mom would plaster my hair to my scalp in the attempt to have slick, sleek uniform braids. That method didn't last long either. More torture ahead. Just cut off my hair and put me out of my misery! I hate the song "I Enjoy Being a Girl."

Life was good for us in the house by the creek. We lived a typical middle-class lifestyle cradled in the years of the late 1950s and early 1960s. Dad worked and hunted and fished. Richard rode his Schwinn bicycle, played baseball nonstop, and tormented me. My mom was a stay-at-home mother and homemaker. She wore her hair much like

Beaver Cleaver's mother and had a clean, crisp apron on when she cooked. We celebrated holidays, cut our own Christmas tree from the mountains near our home, hand-delivered Valentines, and saved our extra change in a large glass piggybank for family vacations. Richard and I would fight over who got to use Dad's hammer to smash the pig and begin the count. I guess you could say these years in the house by the creek were the best rain dancing I remember. The refreshing, pure joy and the relief from the storms reminded me then, and now, about the purpose of my life and all of our lives. Thinking back on these priceless, irreplaceable memories makes me humbly grateful that I chose to try life with its risks, trials, and opportunities.

I smile when I drive by the house that Dad built and the home we all loved. Little did I know when we were living there that Dad would adorn the entire block, almost, with his crafted creations, self-designed, and built homes. The next project would be their dream home.

Count Your Blessings

WE LIVED BETWEEN two mountain ranges. The storms I loved to watch through the sliding glass doors usually came from one of two directions. It fascinated me as I watched the clouds smolder together, turning from light grey to sometimes a dark, frightening black. As the storms conjured their fury, my heart started racing. From watching this scenario unfurl, I required a keen sense as to when I would need to cover my ears. The lightning came first, with its blinding flash that lit up the sky. Then the thunder came pounding through the air with a boisterous presence. The sound reached the two mountain ranges encircling our valley and bounced off each like a silver ball in a pinball machine. The vibrations left their mark on the sliding glass doors that were between me and my world. I felt them shake and tremble beneath my small hand.

The echoing sonic booms of the storms seemed to serve as a reminder of what to expect in the future from Mother Nature. From watching and experiencing these storms in all their fury and rage, I learned that I could prepare myself for the storms ahead.

When we left the preexistence, our loving Father gave us tools to help us prepare for life's storms. One of the most important tools He gave us was His Word, the scriptures.

Recently I attended a sacrament meeting in my ward. A young couple had been asked to speak by the bishop. They were moving from the ward. The young mother began by handing her fifteen-month-old son to his father and gently escorting her two-year-old son to the bishop's wife. Taking a deep breath and relaxing her shoulders, she stood tall at the pulpit, turned to the bishop, and then quickly reversed her gaze to the audience. She apologetically stated that she and her husband had not been given a topic to speak about, and it was frustrating to her. I squirmed in my seat. I rudely thought to myself, which later I regretted, that this would be a talk that I would probably have trouble giving my full attention to and keeping it.

I heaved a sigh as she began. "I decided to speak on my favorite word in the scriptures." I thought, how can you have a favorite word? I have heard of favorite scriptures, but not favorite words. She continued, "I have chosen the word *remember*, because it is always followed by a lesson." Then this vibrant young mother recited a scripture that had me on the edge of my seat, which is where I stayed throughout the remainder of her talk.

The scripture is found in the *Book of Mormon*, Helaman 5:12. "And now, my sons, remember, remember that it is upon the rock of our Redeemer, who is Christ, the Son of God, that ye must build your foundation; that when the devil shall send forth his mighty winds, yea, his shafts in the whirlwind, yea, when all his hail and his mighty storm shall beat upon you, it shall have no power over you to drag you down to the gulf of misery and endless wo, because of the rock upon which ye are built, which is a sure foundation, a foundation whereon if men build they cannot fall."

This is how we prepare ourselves to weather the storms of life. By building a firm foundation of faith in Christ, we are able to prevail against the mightiest of storms. Faith, not fear, is what teaches us how to dance in the rain. Part of having that kind of faith is fostering a positive attitude. Faith has many underlying qualities contained within its spelling: "F" - faith, not fear; "A"- attitude, positive; "I" - integrity, seeking truth; "T"- trust in the Lord; and, "H" - hope for a wonderful future.

One of the earliest lessons on faith that I remember was taught by my mother. It was to count your blessings. Coincidentally it was also the title of her favorite hymn. I was curious to find the meaning behind this endearing hymn and discover the reasons for its popularity.

I found an old hymnbook and reference book used by song conductors. "Count Your Blessings" is not the actual title of the hymn, as I originally thought as a child, but rather it is "When upon Life's Billows."

According to Webster, a billow is a large sea wave; any similar surging mass. One can only imagine the immense varieties of waves that patrol our seas. They can be small, surfer waves or massive destructive walls of water that beat down anything in their path. In life we all have our vision of what our billow is and how we can approach it.

The lines of this particular hymn are intriguing and thought provoking when you take time to read and ponder the words, much like we are encouraged to do with the scriptures. "When upon life's billows you are tempest tossed," a tempest being a violent windstorm or any great commotion or tumult. "When you are discouraged thinking all is lost," discouragement not only can be loss of spirit and hope, but it can also mean that you are obstructed from progression by opposition. "Count your many blessings. Name them one by one," don't just think about your blessings, but write them down and then act upon those blessings. When you act upon or acknowledge your blessings, you are then humbling yourself and enabling yourself to begin to show gratitude to your Maker. The next line of the song emphasizes the benefits of gratitude. "And it will surprise you what the Lord has done," by mentally registering the positive in your life, it uplifts your spirit and causes a deep feeling of great wonder and admiration to engulf you. Fear of the tempest is replaced with faith and hope. You are spiritually able then, and only then, to offer citations of praise to Heavenly Father and worship Him.

The commandment "Love One Another" becomes an intricate part of your being. The Word of the Lord has been solidified with the concept of three, as stated in the Doctrine and Covenants: Section 6, verse 28. "And in the mouth of two or three witnesses shall every word be established." In this inspired hymn we are admonished three times in the chorus to count our blessings and to name them one by one. So many wonderful lessons are in these words. Think about the following verses: "Are you ever burdened with a load of care? Does the cross seem heavy you are called to bear? Count your many blessings; every doubt will fly, and you will be singing as the days go by. When you look at others with their lands and gold, think that Christ has promised you His wealth untold. Count your many blessings; money cannot buy your reward in heaven nor your home on high. So amid the conflict, whether great or small, do not be discouraged. God is over all. Count your many blessings; angels will attend, help and comfort give you till your journey's end."

And then we hear the chorus with the solid foundation of advice given to us through inspiration: "Count your blessings, name them one by one. Count your many blessings; see what God hath done."

The dream house that my parents labored over to see unfold into reality was one of their most precious worldly blessings. This house quickly turned into a home where love was spoken, respect was modeled, and laughter encouraged. It harnessed almost all the memories of childhood, teenage years, and adulthood for me. But it was so much more than an archive of thoughts and memories. It was a part of me and my life. The foundation of values I learned and absorbed while in this home has affected and will affect generations to come with a heritage of positive faith and endurance.

I learned carpentry work at a very young age. Dad and his half-brother, Jay, worked on the house daily. It caused my dad to be away, and I missed him. The house was only half a block away from our apartment, and being the determined, independent child that I was, I made daily trips to check on the progress and work being done, as if I really had any say in the matters. I felt important.

When I arrived, Dad strapped a leather carpentry belt to my waist. Keep in mind that I was only five and petite. He was careful not to put anything in it that was heavy. He didn't want it to throw me off balance and cause falling or injury, so he placed a hammer in my hand and dropped a few nails into the pockets of the belt. The leather was stained and used. When the weather was warm the leather was soft and pliable, but when the weather was cool or cold, the leather became harsh. The pockets stiffened as I placed my hands in them to retrieve the nails, sometimes scratching the top of my hand. My dad gently guided my small hands to place the nail in its proper spot, hold the shaft with fingers on my left hand, and tap the nail head firmly until it stuck, so as to allow me to let go slightly and deliver a more pronounced hit to drive the nail inward. It took several tries, and, yes, I hit my fingers a few times. But the look of pride and love on my dad's face, and hearing his laughter as he threw his head back, made the pain and embarrassment worth it. Dad's eyes would wrinkle at the corners and appear to be almost shut when he laughed. I count the blessing of that memory often. That is one I will always hold near and dear to my heart.

Eventually we started putting the finishing touches on the interior of the home. Mom and I would always sit at the fireplace and cast our eyes to scan over each room and then smile with our approval. My mom's excited squeezes and the fluctuation in her voice made me soar inside and helped me learn about joy and gratitude.

I had been desperately learning to tie my shoes. I carefully concentrated on each step, failing more times than I succeeded. I would look up at Mom and she would just say, "Go on. Keep trying. You can do it."

With that encouragement, I persevered. She left for a while to give her stamp of approval to something in the other room. I was concentrating so hard that I barely noticed her absence. Then it happened. I did it! I did it myself! I looked up to share my triumph, but there was no one around. For a small moment I let discouragement stop my progress and reward. I hung my head and placed it on my knees. Then something surged inside of me and told me to seek my reward. I had earned it. I had to go to my parents and report my success. I jumped from the wooden floor that was still covered in sawdust, brushed off my pedal pushers, and ran to my parents' side, breathlessly announcing, "I did it! I did it! I finally did it." I earned the love and approval of my parents at that moment and experienced a child's innocent joy. I knew deep inside of me that both of them loved and accepted me unconditionally, no matter what. But at that moment in time, it was solidified in my heart in a simplistic way that compared to no other

I believe it is similar to our tempests and life experiences. Our Heavenly Parents are there to give us unconditional love and acceptance. They encourage us as they watch us try and sometimes struggle to accomplish the many tasks we are placed on earth to perform. Our Father never truly leaves us; rather He steps aside and allows us to do it ourselves as much as possible. Then, to understand our reward and blessings, we are encouraged to report to Him in prayer about our accomplishments and communicate with Him to be able to feel of His love and approval. I believe that is how we can measure our progress and grow in faith and gratitude.

Once again, storms and tempests hit, some without much warning. Richard was just approaching his teens and I was six years old when my little sister, Alesa, was born. She was the most beautiful baby. Everywhere Mom would go, heads always turned and gasps and smiles followed. When she came home from the hospital, Mom wanted a picture of Richard and me holding the baby. Mom strategically placed us on the fireplace bench. It was white tile with back trim. The bricks were grey and formed the base of the bench that surrounded the opening of the hearth. As I sat on the tile, I squirmed. It was cold on my legs and bottom and caused enough discomfort that I couldn't hold still.

Mom noticed the imbalance that swept over my little body and my arms that were cradled to accept the tiny bundle. They were bypassed as she handed my sister to my brother. He grinned in triumph at me. That made me angry, so I scooted closer to him and began trying to avenge my dismissal. I grabbed the baby and tried to remove her from his grasp, which did not sit well with my mom. I was chastised severely. Richard and Mom barely caught my sister when she started to slowly slide off Richard's lap. I carried some guilt over that experience. I imagined that if my sister had fallen, I would have been ultimately responsible for the brain damage that could have occurred, the heartache I could have caused my parents, and the money they might have to raise for her treatments. I anguished as a dramatic six-year-old would, but it didn't last long. Pictures were eventually taken and life was back to usual in our family.

I was used to being "Daddy's little girl" and getting a lot of attention. When my sister was born, the attention was drastically deferred to her. My brother doted over her, and I found myself asking him to play ball with *me*, and I soon became the annoying little sister to him. A tinge of sibling jealously ensued but didn't have a chance to develop into a storm. My mom in her wisdom recognized my needs and forged ahead with my performing career and my Shirley Temple days, which diverted my jealousy into a more constructive, positive, thought process. It was also the time that I started to climb trees a lot. Cherry-picking season would always find my brother and me out in the high branches of the Bings helping our dad. Sometimes I would use it as an escape.

Richard and I were assigned chores. Dishwashing machines were not on the market then, and we did the dishes by hand. He washed, and I dried. Mom had us use her dish towels, which actually were white cotton flour sacks. Sometimes they would have a personal touch added to them like an embroidered saying or flowers. They were very large, large enough to grab from corner to corner, twist tightly, and flip and jerk quickly away from a victim. If the victim, who usually was me, was quick enough, he or she could avoid the painful sting the towel would leave as it snapped loudly against the skin. Often it left a red, raised welt. I just remember my brother was skillful at it and did it to me only when Mom wasn't looking. I stood it for a while and then I would run to my retreat, the Bing cherry trees.

I climbed high until I reached the roof level of the house or above. I felt as if no one could find me. I was above reproach.

Sometimes I was in such a hurry to escape that my adrenaline rush carried me to tiny, small branches and reality came to me only after I had settled in the crook of a main limb. Terror would overcome me, and I would hold onto the tiny branches with whitened knuckles, look down, and wonder how I was ever going to get down. It was accomplished eventually when I would recall my dad's earlier instructions while picking cherries. Mom told me much later that she always knew where I was and exactly what cherry tree I had climbed. It seems Mom knew me better than anyone. She knew my dreams and temperament and could predict how I would act or react to any given situation. Dad knew me well, also. His was a different kind of bond, though.

Heavenly Father knows us so well. He knows our dreams, our heart desires, temperament, and is all-knowing about every one of us. Our actions and reactions were predicted from the beginning. We were given our agency. And just like my mother knowing exactly what I was doing, and still allowing me to climb the cherry trees, our Heavenly Father lets us explore and climb our world, both spiritually and temporally.

For about a year and a half before I was to be baptized into the Church of Jesus Christ of Latter-Day Saints, the family had been grossly concerned about my little sis. Mom had a ritual that she would do with the baby every evening. It was pretty typical of mothers in that era of time. It consisted of a warm bath and baby oil or lotion applied before putting pajamas on the infant. A small baby blanket was spread on the living room floor, and after bath, a diaper was applied and the baby was left to kick and move freely. This was the time when the whole family got on their hands and knees and made funny faces and talked baby talk, actually making each other look and sound pretty silly. But Alesa loved it. She would laugh with an infectious giggle that caused all of us to break out in grins.

One night when Richard was close to her face and making her laugh, his smile turned serious and he grew concerned. He looked closer into her eyes. I sat next to him and quietly watched. He then jerked around and asked my mom to come and quickly look. I wasn't sure what they were looking at, because my sister had beautiful big brown eyes that people were always noticing. Mom looked and didn't see anything. Richard said, "Mom, just wait. I saw something. I know I did." Mom looked again, and I will never forget the horror on her face. She turned pale as she motioned for my dad to come and give his opinion. He confirmed what they all had seen. Leaving me sitting by the baby, the three of them retired into the kitchen. Mom cried. I didn't understand. I cautiously leaned over my sister. She kicked her little legs and waved her arms in excitement. I thought when I looked at her that nothing could be wrong with this perfect baby. I grinned at her and I looked closer into her eyes. I saw it too. For a spilt second a small white floating object passed over her dark brown pupil. I blinked to make sure I was really seeing it. The rest is a jumbled blur to me. The atmosphere in our home was not very joyful for the next year and a half.

Much of my parents' time was spent at specialists and numerous doctors in Salt Lake City. All had varying opinions and advice for my parents. They wanted to do what was best for my little sister. Mom and Dad never once forgot Richard or me. We were included in daily prayers offered in my baby sister's behalf. I don't recall those months being void of attention or activity. I still went to dancing. Richard still played ball. We sat around the dinner table for Sunday family time and at night we ate the traditional homemade bread and strawberry jam. I look back on those times in amazement at both of my parents. How could they possibly keep a positive attitude and not let their faith waiver?

Because of one incident that took place in our quiet living room one Sunday afternoon, my testimony was solidified and my concrete foundation with faith in Christ evolved. Not only had preparations been made to prepare me for baptism, but also everyone had been busily involved in Alesa's health and wellbeing. It became a village affair, not just a family one. Concerned neighbors and relatives came over to our home in steady streams. I was seven and three-quarter years old, and didn't pay much attention to anything if it didn't concern me. But this event I remember. It burns in my memory and pierces my heart, bringing humble tears each time I recall it.

My parents had taken my sister to one last doctor in futile attempts to get a specific, desired response, but to their disappointment they were told again and again that my sister probably had cancer and had lost her vision in one eye.

The whole ward held a special fast and prayer for her. The purpose: to evoke the Lord, If it be His will, to make the growth be benign, to make the cancer go away. Well-meaning friends choked at saying the "C" word out loud. The adults liked to use a familiar phrase, "it is in the Lord's hands." Then the Lord would answer your prayers and desires. You could imagine how confusing it was to a seven-year-old who was taught by religious leaders to have faith, pray fervently, and not doubt. I painted myself a potentially self-defeating picture that was black and white, absolute. Maybe I had childlike faith, and maybe not.

It was so very still and quiet. Everyone remained in their Sunday best clothes, with the exception of yours truly. I could not stay in a dress all day long. One by one the older gentlemen of the ward came into our living room. As they entered, they almost whispered, and the atmosphere reminded me of sacrament meeting. I looked down at my apparel and felt ashamed, as if I was being irreverent. It seemed there were a lot of people there that day. But it really was only the Bishopric, which consisted of three men, who actually gave the blessing. (There is that number three again!) A couple of neighbors were there, also. I hid behind the lime-green swivel rocker at the other end of the room. I cowered behind it, hoping I wouldn't be noticed. In better times, it served to be a spinning, tormenting ride of sorts that when I slid off at its end, left me with severe dizziness. I usually lost my balance and fell to the floor, but not that day.

The men and my dad gathered and made a circle, placing their left hand on the shoulder of the man next to him and collectively cradling my sister in their right hands. Two of the men then placed sacred oil on her head to give her a healing blessing. Those words will never leave me. One of them, and I think it was the Bishop, blessed that my sister would be made whole, that she would not have cancer, and that because of the faith of all those who had fasted and prayed, she would continue to grow in health and strength.

I had been sitting with my arms folded reverently and my head bowed with my eyes shut. When I heard that, I immediately looked over at my mother. She had tears streaming down her cheeks and at the same time she wore a faint, relieved expression on her face. I remember that I wanted to jump up and run to her with the good news and cry with joy about our triumph. I felt at that moment, just briefly, that I was the only one who had heard this wonderful truth.

Within minutes the blessing was competed. Everyone shook my parents' hands, and each gently and kindly placed fingertips on the top of my sister's head and said, "Everything will be all right now." They left as quietly as they came and the living room was annoyingly still and somber. I slowly got up from behind the rocker. I really thought that no one knew I was there. Cautiously I approached Mom. "Does this mean that she's better and she doesn't have, you know, cancer, Mom?"

The pause was so long that it made me feel uncomfortable. She didn't answer me right away. It was as if she had to carefully pick and choose her words as to not shake my faith. She then responded, "The Lord knows what is best, and He knows what we can handle. He doesn't cause diseases, and sometimes He doesn't take them away."

I felt like crying. I didn't want to hear that. I became angry. Why didn't my mom believe the blessing and the words that were spoken? I wanted desperately to ask her why we had a blessing for Alesa if it wasn't going to work, but it was not the right time.

That night became the first of many nights where the air became full of my mom's singing, muffled with tears that she so bravely fought back. There was another rocker in our living room. She used it often because it provided a melodic, repetitive motion that would put her children to sleep like a familiar lullaby. This night she rocked and rocked, long after my sister was asleep.

I came into the hall sleepy eyed to see why my mom was still rocking. It was the song, the song she sang that would eventually answer almost all of my questions. Rhetorically Mom sang over and over, "Count Your Blessings." She could hardly get through the chorus without being choked with tears. That song became her foundation of ethical values. She used it for the rest of her life to teach lessons on faith, truth, positive attitude, and hope, all those inner values and qualities we find in the word faith.

A few days later I found myself waiting at the front window, my face pressed against the glass.

I was eagerly waiting to hear what the doctor had said at their visit. Slowly they entered the living room, and Mom settled into the rocker. She began singing and crying, and right then I knew that it was not good news. Dad took me into the kitchen with Richard and told us. It was, indeed, cancer, and she would have to have surgery to save her life.

I hesitated to kneel and say my prayers that night. I was hurt and angry. Maybe, my mom and dad felt the same way. Their adult feelings of anger and disappointment would surely justify my feelings. Wouldn't they? In spite of my anger, my mom's strong influence and teachings caused my knees to bend and my head to bow in prayer that night. I wanted to understand, but I didn't know how to ask for that understanding. I wanted to be comforted, rocked to sleep, if you will, by my mother's lullaby of faith.

Time passed. I was baptized. My sister had her surgery, and I robotically went through the motions of religious rituals that were instilled in my young mind. I wanted desperately to feel the spirit and declare my testimony, but I watched daily my mom's heartache and sadness. I saw wrinkles of worry surround my dad's mouth now, where once there were wrinkles of laughter. I carefully scrutinized their response to everything, like all the truths and values that I had been taught were on trial. Perhaps they were. My parents' example of faith triumphed over any fear or doubts that shadowed our lives.

They went to worship every Sunday, attended the temple regularly, served in any capacity that they were asked, and always had a smile on their face in public and a positive attitude to wear for all to see.

This is why I now count my blessings daily and act upon them. The heritage left me by their examples has become a part of me, such an intricate part that I cannot breathe without it. This is the legacy I want to see handed to my children and their children for generations to come. It is a legacy of survival. It is the rain dance that makes life bearable. Once the storm comes, if we cling to that faith in Christ, we are promised survival, not only survival, but triumph.

I close my eyes when life gets too hard, and I remember the calm that followed this wretched storm. I recall the burning of truth in my bosom as I walked from the waters of baptism and heard testimony from my parent's lips and hearts of the divinity of Christ, our Savior, and how much they loved the Lord. My respect and admiration grew that day toward my parents and never stopped. It continues.

Tools of the Trade

STORMS AND TEMPESTS, used for centuries as symbols, allure provocative thought and teach valuable truths. In Matthew 8: 23-27, the Lord's disciples recorded a time when they were aboard a ship. The Master was asleep in the back. A raging, frightful storm arose and they awoke the Master and pleaded with Him to save them. "And he saith unto them, "Why are ye fearful, 0 ye of little faith?" Then he arose and rebuked the winds and the sea: and there was a great calm." These passages of scripture inspired an intense hymn: "Master, the Tempest Is Raging" where the author pleads for relief from "anguish of spirit" and "depths of sadness."

All of us experience tempests and storms. We need not fear them for they have purpose. Louisa May Alcott said, "I'm not afraid of storms, for I'm learning how to sail my ship." We all chose to build our ship of life and sail its course. We have been given the tools to fashion our ship with skill so that it is strong and durable and it will weather the storms of life. Our lives are centered in our ship, our trade, if you will. We are part of a heavenly family and an earthly family. Our earthly family becomes our trade. A trade is one's regular business, work, occupation, or craft. The Church of Jesus Christ of Latter-Day Saints is engulfed in family doctrines, traditions, development, and support. These tools help us successfully accomplish the development of our trade, our family. One of the most valuable tools given is the *Proclamation of the Family*, read to the world and published in 1995. Many valuable tools are used to craft our ship and fortify our trade each day. Some of these tools come in the form of traditions.

I remember being taught the appreciation for good and whole-some music as I was growing up. I loved the excitement of the stage and performing at a tender, young age. I sang and danced and enjoyed the thrill of musicals on the big screen. As the development in technology grew from black and white TVs and cameras to full color and surround sound, my young mind and heart also grew in knowledge and love for good, appropriate talent.

One of my favorite musicals was *Fiddler on the Roof*. It had great, inspiring music and wonderful life lessons to be entertained. The humor in this film touched everyone's lives. Relatable, deep sorrow was even woven throughout the story. Many related well. One song that stuck in my mind was "Tradition." I was often caught boisterously singing it. This song was sung by the father, Tevjah, who had many conversations with himself and God about these sacred traditions. He convinced himself how important those traditions were for family and religion and how he must stay strong by holding onto them to protect his family and his integrity as head of the household.

Things are not much different now. Traditions are one of the tools that fashion our ship and bond it together to help be unsinkable. They provide the breeze of memory against her sails that allows our ship to pulse through and forward in a storm, and to then melt into the calm. Family traditions know no boundaries or limitations, and their effects are felt for generations.

My mother and father went through another devastating storm before my younger sister Alesa was born. One more child, a beautiful infant girl, was born. She lived only a few minutes and then returned to her Heavenly Father. Her name is Amee Christine. I have no memory of her that I can recall, but again, I watched my loving parents endure this storm with faith and perseverance. In spite of this emergent heartache they did not put on hold the forging of their ship, our family, and they skillfully used their tools of the trade to stay the course full speed ahead.

My family was steeped in traditions. Traditions that came in the form of activities, vacations, work habits, religious rituals, and generally just good times. Most were centered in the dream house that my father crafted with toil and love. It was the house with the sliding glass doors and was my world, my ship, my memories.

Mother was an artist in every way. She molded her art around her home decorating, her cooking, the landscaping, her beautiful appearance, and demeanor. Holidays and birthdays were remembered with vigor and zest. Although we had very little money, we had an abundance of laughter, love, and encouragement wrapped with creativity. As with many average American families, Christmas was a favorite. Preparation began the weekend after Thanksgiving, not before.

My parents always gave thanks and respect for what blessings they had by honoring the Thanksgiving holiday and giving it the time it deserved. During the month of November, deep fall colors adorned our home with scattered turkey and Pilgrim decorations. Christmas didn't emerge until after Thanksgiving, so the weekend after Thanksgiving began the great Christmas adventure and celebration. We were taught to honor our Savior at His birth. Christmas would be celebrated by giving service and love to each other and those in need. We respectfully learned how to balance religion and the traditional commercialism that surrounds the holidays.

The first adventure was the cutting of the family Christmas tree. Dad and my uncle Dean had invested in two snowmobiles. The vehicles were used in winter for their pleasure and the family's use. The yard at the dream house was gigantic with acres of grass in the summer and blankets of snow in the winter. Soon after the first two or three snowfalls, Dad would maneuver his snow mobiling in an entertaining pattern of trails that wound around and through the yard. Later a sled would be attached to the back and we would spend hours being pulled behind the snowmobile. This often attracted the neighborhood kids and sometimes their parents. It was something we never grew tired of doing. The slight, faint smell of fuel and exhaust and the brisk, sharp sting of the cold did not deter us at all. We loved these times.

And so at Christmastime, Dad put his snowmobiles to work. The family made dozens of turkey sandwiches from Thanksgiving leftovers. The turkey was placed on Mom's homemade rolls with a small spread of mayo and a hint of mustard. A few thermos bottles of hot chocolate went along to warm us from the cold.

Off we headed to the mountains above my home. With permit in hand, tools for downing our tree, and the truck carrying the snowmobiles, we went as far up the mountain as possible. The back end of the truck slid back and forth and the wheels spun, which caused my mother to grow pale and squeal, "Be careful, Clifford!" Once the truck had gone as far as possible, the snowmobiles were unloaded. They were pushed off a ramp from the back of the truck onto the pristine snow.

Dean scouted ahead and forged a solid trail for us to follow later. We waited impatiently at the truck for his return. We gazed with anticipation into the bright, blinding light reflected off the snow. It took a few times going from destination to truck back to destination before all of the family was at the spot where the designated tree would be cut and taken home. Even the youngest had a say. After the selection, most of us sat on the snowmobile sipping the hot chocolate and watched in awe as Dad and Dean cut down our Christmas tree. The snow was deep and wrapped around their knees at times. Their hard work was manifested by the large, visible, puffs of air emphasized by the cold. We tied the tree to the snowmobiles in the back of the truck and headed home.

Everyone put up the tree at our house. It was "tradition!" Dad cut and secured it in the tree stand. Sometimes he sprayed it lightly with fake snow, depending on the trend that year. It was called flocking. Then, ever so carefully, we put tinsel, garlands, and ornaments on the tree. The ornaments were kept in a white wooden trunk that had a silver latch on it. Once that latch cradled a padlock. The trunk was fragile and old, especially to hold such valued treasures. Miraculously my parents never had to replace it. It had some memories and traditions of its own, an old toy chest that belonged to my brother. It was a sentimental memory. Some ornaments put on the tree were plain, some frosted slightly with a rough-feeling paint. Most were round and had deep colors of red, green, blue, and gold; some were shaped like a fat icicle. Mom relayed the story behind each ornament as it was carefully and strategically placed on the tree. We would hear of its purchase, the when, how and meaning behind it. It became an enjoyable family history lesson.

The rest of the next week was spent decorating the house, putting up outside lights, and baking for friends and neighbors. My mother was an excellent cook, another family tradition. She learned that skill from my grandmother. As my grandmother grew older, it became harder for her to obtain gifts for all her children and grandchildren, which, by the way, were never forgotten. Grandma made incredible sugar cookies and raisin-oatmeal cookies. For quite a few years I recall getting those as a Christmas present from my grandmother. She would save all her coffee cans, clean them out, wrap them in foil, and then fill them with her flavorful cookies. This tradition of love and devotion has been embedded deep into my soul and memory. The tradition of baking cookies at Christmastime remains unchanged in our family today.

Christmas carried many memories throughout my growing up years. One I especially love took place when Richard and I were very young and Alesa was a baby. Dad had prepared the two of us for our traditional Santa arrival scenario. We had spent most of the evening reading the nativity account from the scriptures and then preparing a plate of cookies for Santa on our way to an early bedtime. Richard and I slept in the same room. We were young and there weren't many bedrooms to spare. I tossed and turned all night long, which annoyed him. I would ask every few minutes, "Is he here yet?"

"No! Go to sleep!" was his irritated reply. At last he finally woke me and we tiptoed into the living room, holding our breath every step of the way so as to promote undetectable silence. We were told earlier to wake my parents, but chose to disregard the request. We proceeded to play with the items that had been left under the tree. Richard received an electric train set, which he promptly put together, and I received a baby doll named Butterball. We were so involved with our newfound pastime that we forgot about my parents. We looked up from our projects to notice them both standing in the hallway and not looking too pleased. Our punishment was to retire our toys to the tree and play with them later.

Our family always woke up early on Christmas morning, much earlier than most. After we had spent time with the immediate family, we jumped in the Buick and traveled to Grandma's house and other relatives to visit and watch them open their gifts. The year I received Butterball, I remember my own child-tempest occurring.

We went to my grandmother's, and I lugged Butterball with me. She was a huge doll.

My grandmother's home was small but warm and hospitable. The furnace was old, and Grandma and Grandpa sometimes required an extra heating device to keep away the chill. It sat on the floor, and I could see the fiery, hot grill from a few feet away. We entered the living room and shook off the snow from our coats and boots. Some of it stayed frozen in clumps on our scarves and hats. We were invited to go into the parlor where the electric heater was located. Most of the folks stayed in the living room, but I boldly ventured into the parlor. After all, I was cold and so was my baby doll. I carefully and tenderly placed her against the heater. A funny smell quickly filled the room. It was one of which I was not familiar.

Suddenly my father burst into the parlor and grabbed my doll away from the heater. But it was too late. The back of her head and her hair were melted off and her clothes were ruined. My small heart was broken. I had made a reasonable decision but did not have the judgment or maturity necessary to avoid the consequences of this situation.

My father picked me up and gently held me in his arms. I soaked the collar of his shirt with my tears. I was devastated and inconsolable. My parents taught me a valuable lesson that day. First, it was just a material thing and could be replaced. It was a blessing that it was not me that was burned and that no one was hurt. Second, it was important to me and therefore it was important to them, no matter how small, so they said they would contact Santa and get Butterball to the doll hospital to make her better. They said I needed to trust them. They loved me and would help make things right. And they did. A few weeks later Butterball returned with new hair and clothes. Of course, I didn't realize that it was a brand-new doll. That didn't seem to matter.

As I recall this incident in my life, what really mattered was that I was taught the value of real versus material. In other words, what I value that is irreplaceable is real and what I can do without is material. Also I learned about the love that my parents have for me and that no matter how small my storm may be, they are there to support and love me through it. I just needed to trust and believe. So it is with our Father in Heaven. He does not care how small our problems are or how insignificant we think they are, He is there for us to love and support us through the storm.

One year I was required, by no choice of my own, to bear incredible pain. My brother had received a chemistry set for Christmas. My parents wanted to encourage the creative genius in him, I guess. It was complete with a microscope that was sturdy and worked well. Richard had explored almost everything that would fit under the scope and had marveled at them microscopically. Then he had the idea that it would be even better to look at blood under the scope. And you can guess what happened next. He held me down and proceeded to prick my finger with the only sharp object he could find, an ice pick. Oh, that hurt! He got in a lot of trouble that year. That was the only Christmas that carried some negative memories for me growing up. Most were wonderful ones that brought our family close.

I remember one year Richard worked at an upscale department store in Ogden, Utah. At Christmastime the store did courtesy gift wrapping for its customers. Richard learned a precise way to wrap presents, including making the corners flat and professional, saving on tape and the time it took to wrap it. He gave us all lessons on wrapping presents so they looked professional. From that year on my dad was designated the official present wrapper, because he was good at it.

Shopping for everyone became a wonderful memory filled with good-feeling life lessons. Mom always spent quality time with each of us, but I recall the shopping. Carefully and meticulously she would make a list of the gifts she wanted to give each member of the family. She taught me that giving with the right spirit meant you took time to think about your gift, select what the person receiving the gift would want or need, and then present it with care and love, which meant it was beautifully wrapped.

Most of the time we had to travel a short distance to accomplish our shopping and it would be an all-day occurrence. We would arrive early to get the best parking place, and Mom would pull out her list from her shiny vinyl purse. After retrieving the list, she snapped it shut abruptly, and off we would go. Often we stopped for lunch. Mom put a lot of love into her traditions, and thankfully they were passed down to me through example. On the way home we always stopped for an ice cream cone at Farr's ice cream parlor.

It was a typical 1950s-style parlor with thick burgundy tile on the walls and large white cabinets. The cabinets had slanted glass on the top to allow customers to see the myriad of flavors from which to choose. I wasn't tall enough to see through the glass; Mom had to lift me up. The attendants wore white aprons that had specks of different flavors on them and a white teardrop-shaped hat on their heads. I always got chocolate in a cup. I did not like the cone. Nor did I like the bun on hot dogs, for that matter. Mother indulged me. She always got cherry chocolate chip and ate the whole thing. Watching mother laugh as she tried to catch the drips of ice cream running down the edge of the cone and reaching over and helping me recover my drips from the edge of my cup was the best time ever.

Food and eating together was a strong tradition in our family. Everyone loved my mother's cooking. She cooked from scratch and rarely followed a recipe. Her methods of measuring were uniquely her own. Living and growing up on a ranch with very little money taught my mother skills that were valuable and that she passed down to me and eventually to her grandchildren. Making homemade bread was one of them. She made it often, and we had hot bread and her strawberry jam every week. Her meals were simple and prepared with love and tenderness. Mealtime was family time. We enjoyed each other's company and really took an interest in one another. Sunday dinners were special and ofttimes consisted of more than our immediate family. My uncle Dean and his family were at our dinner table often, or we were at theirs. This kind of bond is so important in life.

Thanksgiving, a food holiday, was grandiose at our home. Homemade bread, dressing, stuffing, pies, and freezers of homemade ice cream were always expected. My parents opened their home to many at this time of year as well as other times. The living room was filled with four long tables that were set with dark red tablecloths and my mother's best tableware. An appropriate centerpiece adorned the middle of the table, and folding chairs were placed and squeezed together to ensure everyone had a place. Blessings were said and thanks was given, conversations made, games played, and traditional memories cemented to our ship. It's funny how food and smells can bring back memories.

Mom was famous for her chocolate chip cookies, among other things. She would bake them at least once a week, and of course they never lasted long. During my growing up years, it became a competition between my brother and my mother as to who could make them better. Mom always won out, but Richard did get really good at making cookies. Every weekend during high school, friends would gather at my home after games to indulge in my mother's cookies. It made my friends happy, and it didn't hurt my popularity, either. This is another tradition I have passed down. I involved my children in hot cookies after scripture study. I remember my mother telling me that they were so poor when living on the ranch where she grew up that they would ofttimes get only sugar cookies for Christmas. My grandmother had to save the sugar to make them, as it was such a precious commodity. No wonder the cookie tradition meant so much more than just good cookies to my family. It represented love and sacrifice to make someone else happy. In a unique way, it symbolized charity.

The time spent with my mother learning the skills of cooking, canning, and making bread were invaluable. They meant so much more than creating good food and supplying food storage for my family. It was a strong family tradition that cemented the family bond and taught me that learning to be self-sufficient and resourceful would prove to benefit my family and me for good.

Another strong family tradition that was taught was the value of hard work. I held a hammer in my hand and learned how to work at an incredibly young age. I helped my dad with carpentry and with clearing stones from our yard so we could plant grass. I remember shortly after the dream house was completed my father treated himself to a riding lawnmower. My brother had the privilege of taking it for a ride to mow the lawn, and I felt it was only fair that I did, also. So after a lot of pestering, my dad gave in, and I climbed aboard. It had hand controls and a green metal seat. The seat vibrated when the mower was in gear, and it made me itch. But I was determined to show my independence. After a couple of laps around the house, I decided to be brave and mow the back lawn, which would have been fine if the back lawn had been level. It was not. It had a ditch running through the center. The ditch had grass gently growing down the one edge of its sides and up the other, so I really had a hard time judging its depth. I proceeded with confidence.

Next thing I know I am on my side with the mower tipped over and gripping the handles so hard that the mower still wanted to propel forward. Hearing my screams for help, Dad came to my rescue. He shut off the mower, tipped it back up, and then, when he found I wasn't hurt, he burst into laughter. I had damaged his mower, but he still laughed. Needless to say, I mowed the lawn by hand after that.

I enjoyed yard work. My dad taught me that. I hated housework. My mother did *not* teach me that. She taught me cleanliness and life skills and to take pride (the good kind) in doing a job well. My dad would say, "A job worth doing is worth doing well." We had a large garden in the back lot. It mostly consisted of tomatoes, corn, and strawberries. Dad involved all of us in harvesting the fruit and vegetables from our yard. My favorite still remains: picking cherries. There was something magical about being in the top of the trees and taking in the view from there. It was exhilarating to me to savor the accomplishment of the climb to heights never before attained and then to enjoy the tastes of the harvest. Things are not without risks, however. While teaching me the value of hard work, my dad also taught me that you take the risk of possible accidents. He gave me specific instructions on tree climbing to make it safe and decrease my mother's worrying. And I listened, most of the time.

As with a lot of youth, one incident occurred where I ignored my father's teachings and pursued climbing on my own with my own rules. Dad had taught me always to make sure my feet were planted on solid branches that would hold my weight. He said, "Do not go higher than the weight on the branches can hold." I challenged myself that I was going to climb to the top of the tallest Bing cherry tree in our yard. This majestic tree was twice the height of the house and shadowed the playhouse that my dad had built for me. Up I went with confidence and determination. I kept my sights on the top branches and talked to myself to inspire my motivation. The adrenaline was surging through my system. I was inches away from being triumphant when I realized that I had been in such a hurry to be successful that I hadn't taken the time to think about my father's instructions. Then snap! I looked down, and my feet were on tiny, thin branches that could no longer hold my weight. I desperately reached out to grab a sturdier branch as I felt myself embrace the law of gravity. It happened so fast that I didn't feel pain of the fall until I was on the ground. I remember wincing on the way down as my body hit and brushed up against the sharp bark of the branches. I lay there for a few minutes trying to catch my breath and actually wondering if I was dead. Then I saw my mother and father leaning over me asking, "Are you okay?" I replied to them that I wasn't sure, as they helped me up. We determined that miraculously nothing was broken. I had some bruises and some broken pride, but I would live.

I never ignored my father's teachings again. I wish I could be as diligent in following my Heavenly Father's teachings. Why is it that we have to reach a bottom or experience a tragedy before we listen to the promptings we are given by our Father? Why do we choose to ignore His teachings? We are human, imperfect, curious, uneducated, and simply prideful at times. Provided that we can fall without too much injury, our Father is there to pick us up so we can try again and be successful, as long as we listen to the promptings and teachings we have been given.

Spending time together is a priceless tradition. Time is one of life's most valuable commodities. Some of my best memories came from just spending time with my family. It brought opportunities to learn and grow and become close. I learned when I was young how short life really can be, so I cherish my memories of my childhood. They are what makes me who I am.

Vacations come to mind when I think of activities we did together. Mom and Dad would save for months to be able to take us somewhere on a vacation. This sacrifice continued their entire life for their children and later for their grandchildren. We had a fat glass piggy bank that sat in the kitchen on a shelf that we could all reach. We put extra change in it and designated it the vacation fund. When the bank was full, Richard and I had the privilege to break the bank and help count the money. This was done with supervision, of course. Carefully we divided the change and grouped like coins together. Then a family counsel took place to decide our destination. It was simple but meaningful. There is something so genuinely valuable about the feeling of being part of the "big picture." I sometimes ponder on the symbolism of this scenario. We all were part of a similar family counsel to decide our destination eternally. The knowledge that we are children of God, literally, and having the gospel of Jesus Christ lets us feel like we are part of the "big picture." We have our agency to choose how and where we will reach our final destination. Being part of a family has been important from the very beginning.

Our family vacations took us somewhere different every year.

One in particular, I stay focused on in my memory repertoire. I loved to collect rocks, sand, objects that had no value to anyone else, notepads, etc. This family trip took us through Southern Utah. We were on our way to California. Southern Utah is a miraculous smorgasbord of color. Rocks and sand of various hues framed by mountains of sandstone and cedar trees make post-card views. I had a priceless jar that contained my sand collection. When I spotted a different color of sand, my dad would stop and pull the car over to the side of the road. I carefully scooped up just enough to add to the jar to make a colorful layer, one on top of the other. That jar went all the way to California and back to Utah without even being disturbed. I brought it home and proudly displayed it on a wooden shelf in the garage, waiting to find a place for it in my bedroom.

One afternoon I heard a loud bang and the shattering of glass. I ran to see what the noises meant. I stood stone-like and stared at the garage floor. There was my jar of sand, or so it seemed to be, all mixed together with bits and pieces of broken glass. Tears ran down my cheeks. I really didn't know what to do or how to react. When I heard my brother's laugh, I knew who was responsible, and my tears soon turned into anger. Why would he do such a thing? I never found out the answer to that question, but again, my parents used this experience as a teaching tool. After the initial damage control, an apology was given and appropriate punishments ensued. My brother's explanation didn't make me feel much better. "I just wanted to see my firecracker make a sand rainbow." Yeah, right! I eventually forgave him, but it took time. And I decided that sometimes we work so hard to accomplish a task or a project that we want to display or for which we want attention that we fail to recognize it is not the task that becomes invaluable, but the journey of accomplishment.

Family traditions bring on the amazing feeling of accomplishment. For example, the feeling I got when I learned to roast a marshmallow by the fire to a perfect golden brown. Dad cut the willow stick to use as a roasting tool and made sure the coals were hot enough to cook the treat. I anticipated the moment when a glance from him let me know it was time to pull my stick carefully from the fire and gently re-move the tasty treat and put it directly into my mouth. Success! There is nothing like it or like the feeling of accomplishment of learning to catch, clean, and cook a trout. I learned to love and appreciate God's beautiful masterpiece—nature—as I spent many hours camping, trav-eling, and making memories experiencing my family traditions.

Our ship became strong because of family traditions. It brought our family close and provided countless learning avenues. Every holi-day, every birthday was an event to be envied by some and cherished by most. As I look back on my childhood and the traditions I expe-rienced, I think in quiet moments what lessons I learned from each. From coloring Easter eggs, delivering Valentines, and wearing green on St. Patrick's Day to vacations, food preparations, and music prefer-ences, our traditions made me who I am. Traditions form our person-alities and mold our character. There are values woven into the fabric of our existence through the sacredness of family traditions.

I sit at times and let the breeze of memories push me forward with a calm feeling and a slight smile. I feel the strength of the oars of life experiences pushing me into waters that sometimes challenge me but help me grow. I am able to build that ship with confidence and hope and make it safe for the voyage. Every part of my ship has traditions in its framework that were born from values centered in the gospel of Jesus Christ.

Catch a Falling Star

ANCIENT SHIPS NAVIGATED at night using the stars. We still use the stars and constellations to navigate our journey and give us direction. Stars in the universe are without number and vastly unique. They catch one's attention and curiosity. They play with and mold imagination. Captured in art and phrases and incorporated into object lessons, stars play a significant part in each of our lives. A unique star was used by our Father in Heaven to announce the birth of His son, Jesus Christ. The wise men followed this star to reach their destination, the Son of God. Stars can be symbols of hope and heights of goals as in the example of "reach for the stars." They have been used as a reward for good behavior or accomplishing certain tasks. Stars are used to emphasize something or make it stand out. Looking at the massive sky and its blanket of stars on a clear night can certainly take your breath away and humble you. Equally as fascinating is the trail of a falling star when it enters the atmosphere and quickly burns. It creates a majestic orchestration of one of Mother Nature's finest productions.

Songs have been written about stars, beginning with the childhood lullaby of "Twinkle, Twinkle, Little Star." The lyrics were taken from a nursery rhyme written by Jane Taylor and go something like this: "Twinkle, twinkle little star, how I wonder what you are; up above the world so high, like a diamond in the sky. Twinkle, twinkle little star, how I wonder what you are." We are all stars in our own way. We have a destiny, a purpose, and we hope we can provide guidance and direction with our own light and in our own way. Have you ever wondered about who you are and what part you play in the world? Have you ever contemplated your degree of light and to what extent that it allows you to "shine and twinkle," in a sense? I have, many times. I know, however, that I am a unique star. There is no one like me. God has created me and formed me in His own image. I have been given the light of Christ and have the ability and agency to choose to let my light shine for good.

Another song written about a star comes to my mind. This one is about a falling star and written by Paul Vance and Lee Pockriss. It says in the lyrics to "catch a falling star and put it in your pocket. Save it for a rainy day. Catch a falling star and put it in your pocket; never let it fade away. For love may come and tap you on the shoulder some starless night. And just in case . . . you'll have a pocket full of starlight." Sometimes we all become a "falling star." But because of Heavenly Father's love for us, we do not burn out and fade away. We are caught and saved through the Atonement and "put in the pocket of His safe care," and our light is allowed to shine forever so we can reach our destiny and our goal, to return home to live with our Father, Jesus Christ, and our family. Symbolically, when we are caught as we fall and are placed in the "pocket" of the Savior's care, we must all heed the warning regarding our light to "never let it fade away." We must strive to maintain that light, for it will surely be needed to give guidance and direction to ourselves and our loved ones.

Growing up in the house with the sliding glass doors was full of wonderful memories and great life lessons. But as with most of us, there were moments when stars would fall, temporarily, but fall nevertheless. Like the falling stars that we observe on starry nights, some are more intense and vibrant than others. So it is with our falls in life. What matters is that the Savior has paid the price and made the ultimate sacrifice to save us from burning out. Through His atoning sacrifice we can save our light for a rainy day when things look a little better and less cumbersome.

Going into junior high school was both thrilling and painful for me. As most teens do, I struggled with an identity crisis. I didn't know exactly who I was or who I really wanted to be. I jumped around like a ball in a pinball machine, knocking into one object after another. Those objects were making friends; learning to be stylish; taking care of my body; moving out of social awkwardness; trying to please parents, friends, and teachers; and climbing the ladder of likeability. It was really challenging to work so hard at growing up. In my grade school years I struggled with weight, and my brother was mean. He used to call me "chubby checker." For those of you who are too young to know, Chubby Checker was the stage name of a large black man who sang rock 'n roll music in the 1960s. Richard could be such a pest and mean brother, but at the other times could be attentive and adoring to me.

I entered junior high with a weight problem, so I was always on a diet. I hadn't discovered yet that I was a perfectionist. I had an inner drive that pushed me to limits, motivated me to excel, aided in overcoming fears, and allowed me to persevere. Sometimes this perfectionism caused a lot of stress. This stress was part of my weight problem. There were also things transpiring at home that added to the picture. A year before I entered junior high, the Vietnam War broke out. Richard was attending Utah State University in Logan, Utah. He had graduated from high school with an erupting rebellious spirit. He had started to reject my parents' guidance and the teachings of the gospel that he had received at home. Wanting to be a doctor was his dream and goal. Richard was also a perfectionist like me and was over-the-top competitive. Getting great grades became increasingly more difficult as the pressure and fear of being drafted loomed over him. One day, after he had reached a breaking point, he came home and announced to all of us that he had joined the Marine Corps. He said he wanted to serve our country willingly and not be drafted. My father served in the Air Force during World War II, so Richard's joining the Marines was an additional shock, added to the fact that he had dropped out of school.

After digesting the news, we all began to prepare for his departure. I remember standing at the State Capitol and watching him be sworn in to the Marine Corps. It was as if everything was in slow motion. The speeches and the music seemed to drag on and on. Conversation was muddled and hard to follow. Mom kept crying, and Dad was fighting back the tears and constantly clearing his throat to distract himself from the emotions that were surfacing. I watched and observed. I felt sick inside, and I wanted to run up to Richard and give him a big hug and beg him not to go, but I never got the opportunity.

The next time I saw my brother was at Camp Pendleton in California for his graduation. He looked like a wax statue in his uniform. Everything was in perfect condition and nothing was out of place. His belt buckle shined, his shoes shined. It seemed like his face shined, too, but not in a spiritual way. He was more somber and serious. He was more disciplined than I had ever seen him. I missed his sarcasm, smile, and sense of humor. That feeling was only temporary, because it became diminished by the intense sense of pride I had for my brother and for the sacrifice he was willing to make. The last thing he said to me before he left for Vietnam was: "Remember, Jeanne, I'm doing this for you so you can be free and safe." Jeanne was a nickname my family affectionately gave me.

Richard was an excellent marksman. That skill came from all the hunting he did growing up and his perfectionistic attitude. The Marines were going to send him to Officer Training School instead of going directly to Vietnam because he scored so high on his tests and his marksmanship. But my brother allowed his sarcasm to come out in an inappropriate time. He told them he didn't care where they sent him, so they sent him to the front lines to be the battalion's sniper.

My mother never slept well the whole time Richard was away at war. Dad kept busy so he wouldn't have to think about it. Richard managed to write letters as often as he could. I kept all the letters he wrote to me. Most of them were filled with pleas to respect my parents, be good, and be appreciative of the freedoms I had at home. We were told by the Marine Corps that my brother was a hero. He had several medals awarded to him that represented his valiant service to his country.

We learned this information after an arrival of two Marine officers at our home. My mother looked out the front window and watched them approach the house. Color faded from her face, her countenance dulled, and she started repeating the word "No," over and over. We all thought the worst. The officers said that my brother had been severely injured when he tried to save another soldier's life. He had lost his right leg, but was alive. He would be transferred home to a Marine hospital in Oakland, California, soon.

Later we learned that Richard never lost his sense of humor, even when he was serving in a war zone. His commanding officer said that when he was injured, he called for the medic. When the medic arrived he immediately noticed my brother's foot severed from his leg. Richard reportedly stated, "Hey, medic. I need a needle and thread here." He used his sense of humor a lot to help him through his falling-star moments. We went to see him in the hospital. My mother was staring at his leg with somber facial expressions. My brother's comforting remarks were, "No matter how long you stare at it, Mom, it won't grow back." My mother told him to be quiet and then let out a weak laugh, but at least it was a laugh. We hadn't heard her laugh in a very long time.

Richard came home from the war a decorated hero, but unfortunately was not treated like one. He was spit on, called names, and got in quite a few fights. He could never understand why some people did not cherish freedom and why they weren't more patriotic. I just remember the changes that came over him. Anger and bitterness replaced laughter and humor. He was really strong physically, but weakened mentally, emotionally, and spiritually. But this fallen star was a fighter like no other.

I went on to start high school. I became involved in singing, acting, and drill team. I had my first date, which Richard had to screen and approve. I was active in sports, camping, skiing, and golf.

Richard had learned to water ski with an artificial leg. This is a phenomenal accomplishment, because in slalom skiing you have to be able to feel where you place your foot on the ski. He also had become a semi-pro golfer. He insisted I learn how to golf. Of course he was my instructor. He even persuaded my dad to golf.

The war and the memories he carried weighted him down and his priorities began to change. He pulled further and further away from the gospel and my parents. He said he didn't want to be anything like them and wanted nothing to do with the church. Because he had picked up some bad habits while in Vietnam, his situation became more complicated. Those habits drove a wedge even deeper between him and my parents, but it was by his choice that it did. My parents were heartbroken. They felt they were losing yet another child.

Richard left and moved to Denver, where he met a rich society girl and became engaged. Our family was not involved much in the wedding process. Her family felt they outclassed us, and Richard was even embarrassed by us. I don't remember seeing my parents hurt so much. Alesa and I even felt the sting that disappointment and heart-ache brings.

The next couple of years were carefully spent in healing. We tried to stay in touch with Richard and his new wife, but he avoided us. His priority was money and prestige, not family. He found no place for religion, family, or God in his life. His light was fading but not totally burned out.

I had gone on to college, and at this time of my life my testimony couldn't have been stronger. It seemed that the closer I got to my Heavenly Father, the more I suffered from heartache concerning my brother's choices. We all prayed day and night for him. I wondered if he would ever return to his core values and let his light shine again. This period of time tested all of us and our faith. When family ties are strong, you are happy when a member of the family is happy and you also share their sorrows and pain. This is an eternal concept. We are our "brother's keeper," as it tells us in the scriptures. I knew the Lord would answer our prayers, I just wasn't prepared for the answer that would come. I needed to learn to trust in Him completely and understand that He knows what is best for all of us. He loves us and knows us personally.

I was sound asleep when a breathy scream awoke me. It was in the middle of the night. Mom had sat straight up in bed and expressed that she knew something was wrong. She said something had happened to Richard. This was a familiar scene because she had done this the day that he was injured in Vietnam. She had seen the blast that took my brother's leg. This time she didn't see a blast, but rather she felt an extreme sense of doom.

In a few days we received a call. It was the nursing staff at a hospital in Denver. There had been an accident, and my brother was in intensive care. Richard had been with a trainee on a new real-estate run in Aspen. Torrential rain fell. Richard had the trainee drive his car for some reason that day. The roads were slippery and the car had missed a turn and rolled several times. The driver had been ejected with only a broken leg. Richard was pinned under the engine and originally left for dead, but rescuers heard him and cut him out of the car. They rushed him by ambulance to a Denver hospital. He was paralyzed and barely alive. They had placed him on a turning bed with a neck and head brace on. The nurse told us he was stable. More days passed and we eagerly awaited a phone call to hear of any news or progress. It was if we wanted to hear someone say that this was a mistake or that he would fully recover. That never happened.

He finally called. Sounding very defeated and beaten, he proceeded to tell how his wife had become angry about his injuries and accident. She threw all of their wedding china down their stairs, shattering it all, taken money out of the bank, and visited him at the hospital with news. She said she couldn't be married to a cripple the rest of her life, and she was going to Mexico to file for divorce. So much for love, devotion, and wedding vows. My parents did not hesitate in telling him that we would all be there as soon as we could.

You see, we were family. We loved each other unconditionally, as the Lord loves us. No sacrifice was too big to rescue a loved one. So it was with my family. Dad turned his business over to my uncle, we rented our home, Alesa transferred schools, and I followed on a flight as soon as I had a break in classes.

Cleaning up the mess that his wife had left behind took some time, as did making his home wheelchair accessible. We met the neighbors, who were very curious about us. There were lots of visits to the hospital. Everyone sacrificed willingly to help Richard. We loved him so much. We settled into a ward and Alesa made friends at school and church. I spent my time flying back and forth from Utah to Denver. I was in nursing school at the "U" and had to arrange my schedule so I could be with the family.

Eventually Richard could manage and be independent. We all moved back home and tried to pick up where we left off. It was hard. Richard was alone. So I put a plan together that involved an extended stay over my spring break and eventually included the summer months. I was really looking forward to it. I didn't have many ties at the university anyway, and wanted to make my brother a priority.

Learning how to dance in the rain seemed to be my family's talent. Richard had gone through so much as a child and now was faced with extraordinary challenges. He used every ounce of drive to get up in the morning, bathe, get dressed, and fix himself meals. Then he would spend most of his days in therapy at the hospital. The doctors told him that he would probably never walk again, but he was determined to prove them wrong. He worked so hard and he never gave up, or so it seemed.

He had his car equipped with hand controls so he could drive. He would transfer into the driver's seat and then physically lift, with one hand, his wheelchair into the back of the car. Gradually the stress and pressure of his trials began to wear him down. He started drinking and smoking at an increased rate and amount. And then the most pronounced trial of his life happened, an experience that would change his life forever and affect all who knew and loved him.

Again a phone call interrupted my family's lives. This time it was the doctor in the rehabilitation unit at the hospital. Richard had suffered a full respiratory and cardiac arrest. They were able to revive him, but the doctor said he had been dead for seven minutes and they were doing tests to see if there had been any brain damage.

People can usually go five minutes, maximum, under those conditions without having damage. Any longer than five, and the chances become slim or nearly impossible not to have damage of some kind. Days passed and tests were done. At home prayers and fasting took place regularly. A miracle occurred. Our falling star had been caught by the Savior and saved to be able to let his light shine again. Richard not only survived without damage, but he also came back to this life a changed man.

In the following months I made the trip to Denver to stay with and help my brother. So many things that we all take for granted became major projects for him. He insisted on taking a bath every morning. He had to transfer himself into the tub and out when finished into the wheelchair, which took tremendous strength and patience. Then he would get dressed in slacks, dress shirt, vest, and tie, complete with shaving and a splash of cologne. Richard was always intensively meticulous about his appearance.

Eating out was one of his favorites, and while I was there with him we went out to dinner on a three-times-a-week basis. It would always be to a particular classy, expensive restaurant where the staff knew him well and treated him like a king.

It bothered me that he was still drinking so much. He was taking pain medications and other medications that did not mix with alcohol. It became a real problem at home because he would start drinking early in the morning. Then at night he would have night terrors about the war. I remember praying so hard that I could be an instrument in God's hands to help my brother. For observed reasons I felt he didn't want to exist.

Then one day an idea came to me. I felt the spirit was directing me and guiding my actions. To my brother's dismay and shock I asked him to teach me how to make his drinks, and I would fix them for him. He agreed while laughing hard and long about it. The drink he favored was called a Moscow Mule. It consisted of vodka, limes, and ginger beer. I actually got really good at mixing this drink. I was so good that Richard didn't notice that every time I mixed the drink, I carefully decreased the vodka, so that eventually it had no alcohol in it. He was essentially getting a really good fresh lime. He started to feel better physically. When he found out about the drink-mixing ordeal, he was angry at first. But then he realized that I did it because I loved him. I told him that I wasn't going to stand by and let him gradually kill himself. He teared up and offered the smile that I had missed for a long time.

His home teachers paid a visit often to see if he needed anything, and many angels watched over him. We began having meaningful conversations about life. He trusted my unconditional love, and one day I asked about his dying experience. One quiet evening he related to me things that he had never told anyone.

Richard recalled being in a room and lying on a gurney. He said that he remembered having an out-of-body experience where he was looking over his body and the doctors and nurses that were working on him. "It was not painful to die," he related, but "more painful to return to my body." What he told me next cemented my testimony of life eternal, the resurrection and the existence of God and Jesus Christ.

Let me set the scene and share details about the person who met Richard at the veil. I knew my grandparents for a very short time, and so did Richard. We learned that our grandfather Tanner was originally from England and was a stern but kind man. He was tall, thin, and a hard worker. He lived with the philosophy that children were to be seen and not heard. Both Richard and I viewed him with respect and slight fear. I recall hearing what a proud, distinct, and classy man he was. Richard was a lot like our grandfather. Grandfather had deep respect for my grandmother and a soulful commitment to the gospel. He had never touched alcohol or smoked in his entire life. I was told a story about Grandpa that took place in Grouse Creek where he had his ranch. This ranch was the one where my mother was raised. Grouse Creek was a small community with few buildings for social gatherings, so every time a special event was held, it took place at the sandstone church.

My grandfather attended a certain event one evening and drank a large cup of the punch. He drank from the wrong bowl, the one spiked with alcohol. When he returned home he smelled of alcohol and was not feeling well. My grandmother was angry with him and briskly grabbed a broom. With her four-foot frame and strong grip she swung the broom at my six-foot grandfather and chased him to the outhouse, where he was locked inside for the night. My grandfather never touched alcohol or even punch again and still remained strong in the gospel. His respect deepened for my grandmother and they went on to leave a legacy of commitment to God, hard work, and perseverance. Because of my grandfather's legacy of perseverance and testimony, it naturally seemed fitting that this strong, tall, distinct gentleman was the angel that greeted my brother when he passed through the veil into the eternities.

Grandfather arrived on a white horse, and he reached down and lifted my brother up with one hand and placed him on his horse. Richard recalled that things were peaceful, white, and serene. They then traveled to a place where he found himself kneeling beside a white, waist-high altar. The mode of travel or how they arrived at their destination was difficult for him to describe. He said it was as if he shut his eyes, and when he opened them, he and his grandfather were in a different place. Upon the altar lay a large, oversized white, book. A personage stood on the other side of the altar and spoke to Richard. The communication was not verbal like ours but rather through the mind. This person, who Richard did not recognize, told him that this book was his book of life and that it was not finished. The heavenly personage told my brother that he had a mission to fulfill on earth and that he needed to return. It was beautiful and peaceful there. He had no desire to return. He could walk and he was whole. He felt no pain, and he was happy. Knowing what was waiting on the other side of the veil made him resist coming back.

But he recalled then feeling his spirit return to his body. Describing it as the most painful experience he had ever been through, he teared up. Again he felt the pain that a physical, tangible body must experience in this life, and he was breathing and his heart was beating. As he recollected this experience to me, tears streamed down his face, his countenance shone, and he beamed with testimony.

A few months later Richard quit smoking and drinking and he moved back to Utah to be near the family he almost lost. He started showing the traits that were there when he was younger, the traits of determination, kindness, dedication, righteousness, and genuine love that our parents had instilled in us as youth. The Savior had literally caught this falling star and put him in the pocket of His care. Prayers had been answered. Not in the way that we were expecting, but, nevertheless answered by the Lord.

Richard ventured on and continued to challenge the alleged impossibilities that he faced. He learned to play tennis in a wheelchair and became one of the first wheelchair tennis players in America. His picture covered the back page of *Tennis Magazine*, and many local and national TV stations did stories about his tennis talent. More importantly he used his light to guide and direct others. He made tours of the local seminaries and spoke to the young people about his experience of falling away and his miraculous return. Richard influenced many people for good.

Eventually he met and married his wife, who was a nurse in the rehabilitation unit of a local hospital. Their courtship included dinners and dancing. Yes, dancing. She would put her feet on the foot stand of the wheelchair and he would wheel around the room to the rhythm of the music. Later he was ordained an Elder in the Church of Jesus Christ of Latter-day Saints and then married for time and eternity in the Ogden, Utah, Temple. This star's falling had been intense, but after this experience, he was driven to let his light shine brighter and stronger.

While all of this was taking place, a meteor shower was in production in my life. Nursing school was hard, but I loved what I did. I loved helping and serving people. It gave me great satisfaction and a sense of accomplishment. I had been surprisingly social at the university. I involved myself with everything from politics to sororities.

I had a lot of friends and was engaged in every aspect of my life. I went snow skiing every weekend and played tennis and golf. I was getting good grades and experiencing a spiritual high through my attendance at the Institute of Religion. In fact things were going so well that I started to lose track of my priorities. My focus starting drifting away from family and I was attracted to the more prestigious and social areas.

I had auditioned and become a member of the Mormon Youth Symphony and Chorus, which required several hours of my time. I loved singing and preforming, so I didn't mind. I would find myself every Saturday morning down on Temple Square in Salt Lake City at the Tabernacle for rehearsals. One time President Spencer W. Kimball, who was the prophet at that time, came into the practice. He quietly made his way to the alto section where I was seated on the front row. Leaning down he turned to me and asked if I minded that he join us. I was honored to share the alto section with him that day. This was one of the highlights of the long practices that I had while I sang with the choir.

I had a job at a Salt Lake Country Club during the summer and my own apartment. I figured it was time I spent my life away from family and on my own. This was not a wise decision. I started ignoring the promptings of the Spirit and increasingly brushed them off. I lost the guidance that I needed to have God's help in all things. I became prideful and gloated in my successes. Getting dates and attending most of the dances and activities put on by the university and my sorority was not a problem. I also life guarded at the university pool at night for extra money. This drew a lot of attention to me from the athletes who came there to work out.

Even though I was small framed and short, I could hold my own. For instance, I once had to pull a three-hundred-pound football player out of the water because he and his friend were goofing around and he got hurt. The life guarding shirt I wore, which the university had issued to me, fit me like a dress, and I was always being teased and taunted by the athletes to take it off. I think that the baggy shirt gave me the appearance of being helpless and naïve. I never did take my shirt off, and I proved myself to be an outstanding lifeguard. I did, however, make some bad choices and decisions while experiencing university life. Some were comical and some were dangerously serious. The comical ones came because of the reputation that I had acquired on campus.

First, I was short and tiny, and had golden blond hair. And more than that I was hopelessly naïve. I loved people and had a tendency to trust easily. I also had a hard time telling friends "no." So when my sorority nominated me to run for homecoming queen, I reluctantly said yes. I made it to the finals, and I remember feeling a smorgasbord of emotions. Shock and surprise topped the list. Joy and excitement came in a close second. Then came the moment this shining star acquired another reputation and a nickname, The B.C. Bomber. Why? Because I bombed the interview questions in the homecoming queen pageant.

I was on stage in a crowded, enormous room. The student body president of the university was asking the questions. I don't recall what order they were in or where I stood with the other four contestants. All I remember is experiencing the biggest humiliation of my life. My question came, "What do you think of euthanasia, and what is your opinion on how it should be handled?"

My breathing became labored, and I nervously smiled to gain some time while I thought about my answer. It seemed minutes went by before I responded. During those minutes I thought to myself, "I don't even know what euthanasia is, so how can I have an opinion?" I began to panic but thought, "Hey, I'm a good actress and performer, I'll just fake it." Well, that would have been fine, and I probably would have been able to breeze through the tense situation if I had been anywhere near the correct definition of euthanasia. But I wasn't. I heard in my mind, youth in Asia. I responded accordingly. Hotness filled my whole face and the color red became apparently my face makeup as laughter loudly arose from the floor. It was then that I realized that I had made a terrible mistake, a comical one, but still terrible. I didn't think I would ever live it down. To this day my family still teases me about it. I do know the correct definition of euthanasia now, though. This experience was funny and embarrassing, but worse it also drew attention to my naivety. This was a negative result of that experience.

Weeks after homecoming, a man at the country club began flirting with me. He was the bartender and would bring me Diet Cokes with lime. With every drink came an invitation to go out with him. He didn't have the standards that I had been taught to seek in someone to date, so I told him no every time. Then he badgered me by bringing religion into the picture. He would say that I was prejudiced against him because he wasn't a Mormon and that I didn't think he was good enough for me. I tried to be nice to him and at the same time stand my ground. But I gave in to the enticement of Satan. Satan bombarded me with thoughts of guilt, thinking I was better than this guy. And I enhanced Satan's influence by having the attitude of appeasement, thinking, "It's only one date. How can that make a difference? It won't matter." I finally gave in to temptation. I accepted his invitation to go to a movie, thinking that should be fairly safe; there would be a lot of people around. This thinking seemed to justify my decision. My lack of judgment and naïve trust got me into a situation I had been warned about by parents and church leaders.

The date came and was uneventful. I remember feeling anxiously uncomfortable with him. At its end we arrived at my apartment, and I discovered that my roommates were not at home. When he discovered this fact, he forced his way into my apartment and assaulted me. I fought him with all my strength. I frantically kicked and scratched, but that action was met with the wincing pain of forcefully being held down to the floor. It happened quickly and things became a blur. I didn't even remember when he left or how I got to my room. I do recall sobbing and crying so hard that I felt paralyzed. This star had fallen, and fallen hard.

I can't begin to express the devastation I felt, the humility I experienced, and the guilt I brought on myself. I had ignored the promptings of the Spirit. I needed God's help, but how could I turn to God now? I attended singing practice at Temple Square the next day. Everyone could tell something was wrong. I couldn't hide it very long. I eventually told my parents, my best friend, and my Bishop. Concerning this unfortunate incidence, I found out that I was part of a contest at a fraternity to see who could get me to go out with them first. I was horrified to learn that I became a notch on that guy's bedpost. I cried and cried until my chest hurt. I had frequent panic attacks and often gasped for air.

The healing process did not begin immediately. I wanted to be punished because I felt I had made such bad decisions. I had convinced myself that I got what I deserved and could never be forgiven. But I was wrong. It was in the time frame that lay ahead of me where I would feel the Savior catch me and put me in His pocket until I could gain the strength to "never let it (my light) fade away." Because of His unconditional love and the support of family, I gradually healed, not completely at that time in my life, but later. My light would shine again, and shine stronger.

You see it's all about family. Our eternal family and our earthly family. The love generated by both can help us vault over the highest obstacles. One afternoon my sorority sister came and got me from the chapter room of the house where I was deep in studies. She said that someone at the door was for me, a really handsome man with two dozen roses. She asked if it was my boyfriend, and I said no abruptly, because I didn't have one at the time. I slowly approached the door and cracked it open. I had no trust for men at all. There sat my brother, Richard, in his wheelchair with two dozen white roses cradled in his lap. I helped him inside, and he handed the roses to me. He said, "I love you, and in my eyes you are always as pure and clean as these roses." I asked him how he got up to the house, because the street was abnormally steep and there were several stairs to climb to get to my front door. He responded by telling me that eight nice, strong students came and helped him up the stairs. Through my tears I could see his great and wonderful smile. I gave him a big hug and then we went to lunch, just like old times.

Sometimes when we fall it takes time to heal and to fully appreciate the Atonement and what part it plays in our lives. I had always thought the Atonement was for sins that needed to be forgiven. I realized at this time in my life that it meant much more. The Savior knew my pain and He felt it and all the humility that I felt. I was embarrassed to turn to my God because I felt I had let Him down. The knowledge that my parents had instilled in me as a young child that I was a child of God and had divine potential was what grounded me and eventually allowed me to invite the Atonement into my life. I allowed it to help me heal. I also learned how important it is to forgive yourself and progress forward while still staying focused on the future and the goals you want to obtain. My rainy day was upon me, and I needed that light to help me learn to dance in that rain.

Many storms came during my college years. There were also great accomplishments. I graduated from nursing with honors, continued to sing in the Mormon Youth Chorus, pursued my athletic passions, gained back the self-respect that I had temporarily lost, and grew in my testimony of the gospel in a way that I never thought possible. I understood what it was like to make mistakes and still be loved unconditionally and be forgiven. Hurting and healing are both processes. One precedes the other. The Savior can help with both processes if we allow Him to do so.

The day of graduation came quickly and with much anticipation. A few days before this event, my parents had left to go to Fillmore to see my sister, Alesa. She attended Girl's State, and they wanted to see her graduation. On the way down, they were involved in a car accident. An older driver who was pulling a trailer on the freeway decided he was going the wrong way. He pulled a U-turn and blocked any possibility of my dad not hitting him. Dad tried to make the collision have the least amount of impact and damage as possible. It was unavoidable.

I received a call from the Highway Patrol. I was told that my mother was in critical condition, that she had been thrust through the windshield and had a broken arm, pelvis, and right leg. They were going to transfer her to a larger hospital in Ogden the next day. My father was in shock and was also being treated. My sister called a few minutes later and said she was getting a ride up to my apartment and then we could decide what to do.

Before I set the scene for what happened next, I need to explain the journey I had been on and describe the storm that had lingered overhead. A year before graduation I had met a young returned missionary at an institute dance. He courted me and we dated for a period, and then we became engaged. I was still suffering from low self-esteem and was still in the process of healing. But I made this decision a subject of much prayer. We were married in the Ogden Utah Temple. A few months into the marriage I became pregnant with twins. I began listening to the Spirit on a daily basis more so than I ever had before. I felt a strong sense of uneasiness and things seemed unsettled. He started ignoring me and emotionally abusing me. It was as if I wasn't a part of his life. Because I was pregnant, my emotions were always at the surface, and I was also trying to graduate from nursing school, so life was intense.

One day I came home to my apartment to find him gone. He had been downtown and filed for divorce a few days before my graduation. Any kind of contact with him became futile. I desperately called his family members to try to talk to him or get some kind of explanation. I was met with cold, rejecting responses to my questions, but none were ever from him. He wouldn't talk to me. I didn't know why. I couldn't decide if my nausea that I was feeling at that time was from my pregnancy or from the developing situation.

These two major events happened within two days of each other. I was not only facing storms, I was headed into violent and ravaging currents. I didn't know what I was going to do. I prayed. I cried. I questioned.

My sister arrived in time to attend my graduation with me. I updated her on my latest situation and she updated me on our parents' condition. I felt numb at graduation. I barely managed a closed, weak smile when I received my diploma and faintly heard the applause to acknowledge my accomplishments. My husband had the audacity to attend my graduation. I caught a glimpse of him staring down at me from the balcony. My wise sister quickly grabbed my arm after the graduation had ended and whisked me away to the car.

We then traveled to Ogden to visit my parents. Quietly I entered my mother's room. She was heavily sedated. Dad was sitting in a chair with his head hung low and looking extremely concerned. We gently asked Dad to recall the events that brought them to this point and place. We were interrupted by a nurse who was inquiring about me. She said that a man wanted to see me. I described my husband to her, and she confirmed that it was he who was asking about me. I got up to leave the room to see what he wanted and had to motion to my sister to wait there for me.

I remember approaching him with a sick feeling and pounding heart. He merely handed me some documents and said, "I'm sorry; it's me, not you." He had his demons that he was fighting, same-sex attraction, and felt he needed to walk away from our marriage. He did exactly that. I did not have the strength to call after him or the breath even to talk. I turned and slowly walked back to the room. I had not had the chance to tell my dad about my situation, and my mother was sleeping under sedation. But my sister knew and grabbed the documents from my hand and in horror exclaimed, "I can't believe he came here to do this!" Directed explanation to my dad followed, and then, when I thought the storm could not get worse, it did.

I began to miscarry. I was experiencing severe abdominal pain and bleeding. My sister rushed me to our hometown hospital, where I lost the twins. I was numb and emotionally unresponsive. I had a surgical procedure done and then was hospitalized with restricted visitors. My sister returned to my parents and family members came and sat with me. I had never felt so alone.

The next few months were again spent in healing. I reached to the deepest place inside of myself to pull the strength that I needed to go on. I felt extreme loss, abandonment, depression, and physical weakness like I had never felt before. Again it was family standing by me and the prayers that were answered that helped me weather this tumultuous storm. I did not understand the whys, but my faith in God and knowing that he loved me deeply kept my light shining. Church members helped after my hospital stay and my parents' recovery. Life went on. Again I watched my remarkable mother and father rebound from the destructive forces of the Adversary.

You see, six months before these intense and tragic events took place in my life, my brother Richard passed away in his sleep. It happened two days after Christmas. His wife had tried to revive him, but was told by my brother's voice to let him go. His voice told her that he had finished his mission and was called home. My brother, once a falling star, had been permanently kept in the Savior's loving care, and his light would eternally shine in heaven. I watched again as my parents experienced another devastating loss. Nothing compares to the loss of a child, no matter how old or young they are. Richard was only thirty years old. He had been married a little more than a year. His life left a legacy of hard work, perseverance, and love of God. My parents' hurt could not be described, but their undying faith and testimony could. You could see it by their actions, their countenance, and the way they lived their lives. These wonderful people, my family, are what helped me survive through my falling star phases of my life. Truly stars in our family had fallen, and those stars had been caught by the Savior. They had been carefully and lovingly put in the pocket of the Savior's care, and their light was saved for a rainy day.

No matter what we go through in life, no matter how hard it becomes, we must remember the Atonement of Jesus Christ and the beautiful part it plays in our existence. We must find comfort in knowing that He has and will catch us when we fall, and He will not allow our light to burn out, but rather to grow in intensity and shine brightly to be a guidance and an influence to those around us. Hurting and healing are processes. They both take time, patience, and faith.

A Thing Done

HAVE YOU EVER been frozen at the doorway of a building where you were about to make an exit, when a violent cloud burst stopped you at its edge? One hesitates to go out in such raging storms. We have the inconvenient thoughts lingering in our heads of getting soaking wet, ruining our clothes and belongings, or even more dramatic, being struck by lightning. I have found myself in these situations. My thoughts spin in my head debating and arguing about the debacle while trying to find an immediate solution to the problem. How do I move forward without the effects of the storm enveloping me? Sometimes we waste a lot of time in debating matters, ones that might have several solutions. Boyd K. Packer, president of the Quorum of the Twelve Apostles, made this statement about storms: "Somebody has to stand, face the storm, declare the truth, let the winds blow, and be serene, composed . . ."

After the intensely tragic events of my college years, I burst through the door into the rain and storm, facing the consequences and all it entailed. I wanted to make something of myself and give my life meaning. I wanted to move forward, heal, and progress. My mother had instilled in me a positive attitude and a vision of faith. My brother left a legacy of perseverance. My father taught me to work hard and be ethical. He had a saying that I adopted: "A thing done when thought of, needs no further attention." It proved to be a guiding principle when making my decisions. Wisdom weaves through each word of that saying. We need to take time and utilize prayer in our decisions. We need to remember that God gave us a brain to use and agency to facilitate our progress forward. When we reach a crossroads or we hesitate just a little, sometimes it is better to just do it than to waste time debating or pining. The prophet Joseph Smith said, "When the Lord commands, I just do it." I strongly believe that because we are children of God we are destined for greatness. We are not sent to earth to fail, but to grow and progress and to reach our divine potential. We are to have joy, the joy that comes through keeping the commandments and doing our best to live a Christ-like life.

So standing at the door, looking at the raging storms and torrents of rain outside and knowing I need to move forward to get to my destination, I do something that "requires no further attention, when thought of." I count to three, say "Go," and burst through that door. I am interestingly composed and serene because I am armed with the knowledge that with God, nothing is impossible. I know that I will not face this life alone. And actually the rain causes some laughter along the way and refreshes me.

My life became the way to move forward. I met a young missionary who also sang and was athletic like me. We had everything in common. He didn't judge me about my past and never looked at me as "damaged goods." I began to laugh and feel good about myself again. It took a lot of coaxing by friends to find the courage to date again, but I did. I stayed active in church and attended the Temple as often as possible. I involved myself in my profession, nursing, and loved it. I wrote several songs. They included both the music that I played on my guitar and lyrics. I served in a calling at church, and my Heavenly Father was at the helm of my happiness. He guided and directed me forward. The Atonement helped heal me, and I was extremely blessed. I developed a humble attitude of gratitude. I sincerely wanted to become what I was meant to become, a righteous daughter, mother, and wife. I didn't know exactly what my future held, but I was getting better and better at dancing in the rain. I packed my whole being with anticipation of what was to come.

After a spirited courting period, a creative and flamboyant proposal ensued. It took place beneath the feet of the statue of Christ on Temple Square in Salt Lake City, Utah. The visitor's center was across from the beautiful temple where we would be married in a few months for time and eternity. Due to circumstances from my first marriage, I was able to receive permission from the First Presidency to be sealed in the temple again. I received a wonderful letter from President Kimball wishing me joy and happiness and encouraging me to keep my covenants. I cherished his council. It was the letter that became a beacon of hope, one that I needed at that time to be able to stand and face the storms ahead.

I truly believe that everyone who works hard, sincerely repents, and wants and desires to do good deserves a second chance. I had been given a second chance. My heart was full of gratitude, my soul was soring with anticipation, and my countenance was illuminated with the hope of a bright future and the chance for true joy. I engulfed the freshness that one smells and feels after a rainstorm. I could see the clouds gradually melting into the distant past and the hopeful light ahead of me. I had fallen deeply in love. Love has a way of making life exquisite. It challenges the hesitant, motivates the tired, calms the anxious, and uplifts the downhearted. I was ready. I felt like a child once again anticipating the thrill of the next rainstorm or the new adventure just around the corner.

Getting your life started as a new couple can be exhilarating. The world presents young brides with many choices and decisions. I remember the beautiful gown my aunt made for me. She spent hours each day hand sewing beads to the front of it and along the sleeves. She lovingly made my veil that had special lace along its edge. So much happiness was shared with my entire family, friends, and neighbors. I gave my heart and soul to the wedding preparation, including writing a song for my newfound love. But with all the wonderful and colorful trimmings of commercialism that went with the planning and reception, the memory that I cherish to this day was the sealing ceremony in the Salt Lake Temple. The Spirit was strong, the love undeniable, the light brilliant. I took in every word and savored it. I gazed into eternity with hope and a solemn, sacred, serious commitment to my covenants and the promises I made that day. I felt the presence of our future children. I cried tears of joy. My heart was full.

All young couples begin life together with elevated expectations of living out their dreams. We were no different. We soon found that marriage takes work, commitment, and compromise. It was important for us to remember to put God first and then each other. It just felt right. Life was good. We prayed together, read our scriptures together, laughed, and cried together. We learned to compromise and work as a team with Heavenly Father at the head.

Our first apartment was historical. I remember the day that President Kimball got the revelation to restore the priesthood to every worthy male. I was standing in my living room. I dropped to my knees and began to sob with tears of complete happiness. It was here, in this tiny first apartment, that I voyaged into the waters of learning how to cook, clean, and manage a household.

Planning together and working hard enabled us to buy our first home eventually.

It was an older home that was built strong and sturdy. It had antique charm complete with lots of beautiful wood trimmings and a fireplace in the living room that was adorned with a mantel that ran the whole length of the wall. A large porch surrounded the front of the house. I spent hours sitting and playing my guitar on that porch. A small wooden garage was out back and a strip of dirt that once housed a flower bed cuddled the wall by the back door. It would eventually be home to my tomato plants. The kitchen was small, but we didn't need much. Two bedrooms were found on the main floor. The smaller one immediately was designated as the future nursery.

One bathroom adorned the hallway. The fixtures in the bathroom were eighteenth-century style, complete with a freestanding sink and an iron claw tub. It was perfect! It was home. We worked hard and completely finished off the basement and turned it into an apartment. Later we rented it to my sister and a few other university students. Our neighbors ranged from President of the Church of Jesus Christ of the

Latter-day Saints David O. McKay's secretary to some unfriendly men who hung bags of marijuana down their chimney. They made me a little nervous. Needless to say, the neighborhood was diverse.

Our first Christmas was among many firsts that took place in this home. We had a real Christmas tree that welcomed you with a burst of fresh pine scent as you opened the door. We built our first fence. I gave my first guitar lessons to several promising students. And the most important first, our first child was welcomed into the world in this home. He took his first steps in the living room by the Christmas tree. I cooked my first gourmet meal in this small but sufficient kitchen. I canned my first tomatoes and peaches, made my first loaf of homemade bread, crafted my first homemade Christmas tree ornaments, and attended the first family ward. It was also the place of our first major storm as a married couple.

Some storms come on abruptly and give you no warning. Others seep into your life gradually, cunningly leaving hints of a warning or crumbs of clues to forecast the pending tempest. I noticed some of those hints and crumbs when my husband started to change spiritually. The prayers got fewer and scriptures weren't read as often. Irritability and defensiveness set in. Fault finding became a pastime, and the light dimmed in his countenance.

We all have our demons, fears, and challenges. In marriage I believe strongly that they can be faced together with faith and love. But first you have to recognize that there is a problem. You have to go to the Lord with a humble, repentant heart. If that does not happen, a cancer can develop, a deadly, devouring cancer that can allow Satan in to destroy love, progress, and character. Cancers come in all forms: addictions, law breaking, stealing, or other forms of sin. When our value system is founded on the rock, Jesus Christ, firmly and soundly, we have a better chance to curtail these cancers. When our foundation is weak, we are at risk to succumb to the evil one and allow the cancer to grow undetected, until it reveals symptoms of destruction. Pornography is one of those evil addictions that can cause these cancers. It was my husband's biggest demon. It was also responsible for starting a terrible storm in my life that eventually destroyed my marriage.

Lessons can be learned from facing our fears and demons. There is a beautiful painting of the Savior standing at a door. There is no handle to let Himself in, but rather entrance must be initiated by the one on the other side of the door. This painting is symbolic of the principle that Jesus Christ is there for us, but we have to ask for Him. We have to open the door and let Him in. His Atonement can heal only when we allow it to heal. And so I prayed and waited for my husband to ask, to let Him in. I prayed valiantly and with determination that God would answer my prayers to turn his heart around and fix things. I honestly felt and believed that God would answer my prayers, because they were righteous desires for my family and myself. Prayers are not always answered in the way we feel they ought to be answered.

Through this tumultuous, unkind, and painful storm I learned an extremely valuable lesson. One of the most priceless gifts our Heavenly Father has given us is our agency. In the preexistence, Satan was the one who wanted to take our agency away and make us choose the right path. He wanted all the glory for himself. Jesus Christ proposed a different plan. He wanted us to choose for ourselves, and He wanted all the glory to go to Heavenly Father. He became our Savior to atone for the sins and mistakes that He knew we would make, because we would not be perfect in utilizing that agency. The Lord showered down on me His tender mercies and patience by teaching me an invaluable concept about agency. You cannot ask the Lord to take away someone's agency. Agency is a gift that is nonrefundable. By praying that God would change my husband and help him see the errors of his ways, I was essentially asking the Lord to take away his agency and "make him do what was right," which does not happen, no matter how righteous our desires are.

Change comes to a person through repentance, love, forgiveness, and a desire to change for the right reasons. It took a long time for me to completely accept this lesson. I lived the next thirteen years waiting for that change, praying for strength, and nurturing a broken heart. I felt the uncertainty of hopefulness and then disappointment. I moved forward by staying focused on my values and beliefs. I relied heavily on my faith and the teachings of my childhood. A prayer was constantly in my heart. Heavenly Father came close and talked to me through inspiration. He gave me strength. The Atonement of my Savior took on a whole new meaning, again.

While my husband was fighting his demons and addictions, life still moved forward, as it should. Happy and rewarding times were ahead of us, and five of the best reasons for moving forward were born into our family. These five children became the core of my very existence. We soon moved from our first home. We moved back to my hometown, a small rural community where everyone knows everyone, which can be an asset or a detriment, depending on your perspective. I always considered it an asset. I loved my hometown. I had family there who became my life-giving support system. The move was to be our fresh start, our new beginning. We thought the demons had been conquered and the storm was settling.

We comfortably settled into the "Mormon family culture." We were active in church. Our callings were influential and came with big responsibilities. Valiant efforts were made to have Family Home Evenings, attend the Temple, pay our tithes and offerings, and have regular scripture study and family prayer. We participated in our community's events. Both of us coached athletic teams for our children and were very involved in their lives. I juggled PTA, Primary Presidency, coaching softball, monitoring dance competitions for my girls, and working part-time as a nurse. My husband was equally as active. He was magnetically charming and was liked by almost everyone. Entertaining guests and friends was one of our favorite things to do.

One particular event I remember fondly was an adult Halloween party held every year. We had been in three different wards and had moved only once, which was a few blocks away. In each ward we made new friends and always invited all of them to the Halloween party at our home. It was a costume party, and we had a pumpkin-carving contest complete with prizes. Potluck food was the main event, and the party was topped off with a hayride and hot apple cider. Many fond memories were made and bonds of friendship sprouted. This tradition continued until our second son was born. He came into this world the day before Halloween, which put a stop to our annual Halloween party. From that time forward, the holiday became his very own, and we made sure he felt special by celebrating it with him at its center, not us.

I recall many wonderful times in our new home. Most all of them were centered on my children and extended family. I pushed myself to achieve to my limits and spend every precious moment I had with my children. They became my sanctuary. I could escape the pain and heartache I was experiencing in my marriage by focusing on my children. My husband and I spent many hours in counseling. I sought advice from ecclesiastical leaders and my wise parents. All I ever dreamed of was to have a family and a marriage like my parents, a marriage based on love and trust; a forever, eternal marriage.

Sometime during the journey the demons my husband once fought returned. They crept in gradually and ever so subtly. I think now that perhaps they never left completely. Now those demons and his choices affected not only me but also our five beautiful children were equally affected in a negative way. I saw a few signs that warned me of the danger that was ahead, but I was determined to stay focused, to ignore the troubled marriage, to ignore the verbal and emotional abuse, and to stay in my comfort zone of denial. Why? Because I had five children, I had received covenants in the Temple, and I loved my husband and wanted to have the kind of faith that would promote a miracle and calm the storm.

I begged for the Lord to step in and soften my husband's heart, to change his mind. The pornography had led to infidelity, and consequently he decided that I was no longer considered to be his eternal companion. When that was said to me, I felt the life seep from my soul. Concentration was no longer my friend. My chest hurt because my heart was pounding so hard. I could not stop crying. I cried so hard that I gasped for air. This was the initial response. What followed was shock and a stunning mode of limbo. The only things that kept me sane were my children and my determined persevering mentality.

After all the counseling, talking, praying, and talking some more, the situation did not get better, but worse. He had his agency and was using it in his very self-centered way. Nothing would take that agency away. Marriage takes two partners who want the marriage to succeed. Marriage takes trust and unconditional love. Marriage works when God is at the head and part of the triangle. I kept hanging on to those concepts in hope that they could still be a reality. Then the storm hit, and hit hard.

I had been to a professional basketball game with my sister. She had taken me to it for my birthday. My children were with my parents. When I arrived home, I found my parents at my home with all my children sitting together on the couch. They had nauseated looks on their faces, and their countenances were pale. After questioning my oldest son, I discovered many things missing from my home. Items of value, both sentimental and monetary, were gone. My husband's clothes and personal items were gone, but more importantly, he was gone. Neighbors said that he had loaded a flatbed trailer up while I was away. They said they thought we were moving. That was the longest most painful night of existence I have ever experienced. The months ahead could be described as ugly, painful, and deadly. The man I loved and who was the father of my five children had abandoned us and destroyed our family. Oh, this was not a storm I was ready for at all.

I worked three jobs to maintain a decent lifestyle and be able to keep our home. My mom, dad, and sister literally helped me raise my children. I struggled to have Family Home Evening because there was not a father present. I cried whenever I attended the Temple because I thought of the sacred covenants and vows that were made there. Praying for things to be different consumed me. I was used to having the necessities and all that we needed. Now we were faced with near poverty and needing to turn to the church for help. We were blessed to have the gospel in our lives and such a supportive family. As hard as these times were, so many valuable lessons were learned.

First of all, I learned about humility and being able to let others help me. I learned about service and how it helps lessen the sting of sorrow. I drew closer to my Savior and realized I could not do this by myself and that I was truly not alone. I felt my Lord's love deeply in His tender mercies toward me and my children. The beginnings of forgiveness took hold ever so slightly. I knew it would take time and a lot of work for it to be complete and genuine. I learned to fashion my prayers differently by putting the Lord's will first, not mine. This is something I hadn't been doing. I had not put myself in the Lord's care and accepted His will. My desires were so strong that they curtailed humility and contriteness. And I learned to value and respect agency. I grasped a deeper understanding of the Atonement and allowed it to help me heal. Healing didn't come right away. I fought the divorce. I didn't want it. I prayed for things to change. I sought out blessings from my stake president. It wasn't until I experienced some personal revelation that my attitude and perception of the whole picture was altered for good.

One night I had finally dropped into bed after an exhausting day at work and after doing nightly rituals with my children. I said my prayers, but not with as much vigor as usual. I remember how cool the pillowcase felt against my face and the peacefulness of slipping into sleep. Then I sat straight up in bed. I was perspiring and my heart raced. The dream or vision or whatever it was I just had brought tears to me, and I began to sob uncontrollably.

The vision was as follows: My family and I were standing on a ledge that overlooked a deep gully. Everything was blackened, as if there had been a fire. Smoke was smoldering and the sky was dark and eerie. I leaned a little closer to the edge to get a better look. When I turned around to say something to my children, my husband pushed me over the ledge. I grasped at the rocks to keep from falling. They were sharp and painful, and I felt them scraping my skin. Fear was motivating my strength. I tugged at the rock wall with both arms as hard as I could. My five little children reached down and pulled me up to safety. I bent over to brush myself off and at the same time abruptly asked my husband what he was trying to do. He lunged at me as if to push me off again, but I jerked away from his grasp. He fell forward down into the ravine. I watched in horror. There was no way to save him. I suddenly felt a deep loss and sadness. I thought of my children and what they must be feeling. I turned to comfort them, but comfort was not needed. They were happy and smiling. Our dirty, sooty, clothes were perfectly white. Green grass and blue skies surrounded us and framed the wild flowers that speckled the entire area. We embraced, and I felt a love that a mother rarely feels, one of peace and security and hope. This vision repeated itself for the following three nights. The details did not waver or vary. It upset me a great deal. This was not how things were supposed to end! It was not the answer I wanted. "Why can't things be different?" I pleaded with Father in Heaven while tears stained my cheeks. The fourth night I put a call into my stake president. I needed to see him.

My stake president was fully aware of my circumstances. He gave me a blessing after hearing me recount the vision of the last three nights. I was counseled by him to know that the Lord was answering my prayers. He interpreted my vision to mean that the Lord did not want me to stay with my husband. My stake president said that my husband would bring me and my children down if I stayed with him. And further, the only way we could be happy and partake of the Temple blessings was to let him go. I was to give him a divorce and move on with my life. This advice was not regular or routine, but because of the vision the Lord had intervened on my behalf. Then my stake president gave me scriptures to read in the Doctrine and Covenants. This was a turning point in my life. I finally turned myself over to the Lord and asked only that His will be done and that He would give me the strength to get through this trial, this horrible, devastating storm.

Things were rough. I still went in the bathroom at night, shut the door, and turned on the shower for noise. I didn't want my children to hear me sob and yell with frustration into my hands to muffle the sound. I had to be strong. I needed to take my stake president's advice and listen to the Spirit. I proceeded forward. "A thing done when thought of needs no further attention."

It Is What It Is

A STORM IS something that we can't change. It is what you see, feel, and experience in your own unique way. I have often in my life encountered some interesting sayings. Some are quotes by family or friends. Some are derived from famous political, historical, or religious leaders. And then there are those that are fabricated and woven from our cultures and traditions. "It is what it is" happens to be one of those. Many diverse groups lay claim to it. But with the aid of modern technology, I found that there is not a specific origin. It can be interpreted in several ways. It can represent a certain frustration and resigned acceptance, answer a question that can't be adequately answered, or indicate to move on and not dwell on a past that can't be changed. I believe the storm of destruction that hit my marriage took on all three possibilities. I was frustrated that I had to resign myself to acceptance that I could not change the face of the storm. I had to put to rest the question "Why me" or just plain "Why." Those answers did not come immediately. And thirdly, I needed to move on and not dwell in a past that could not be changed.

Aren't we all faced with these challenges in our lives? Do we not feel paralyzed to forward movement when we resign ourselves to the thought that things can't be different? These are tools of the Adversary. It is good to recognize the situation for what it is, learn from it, and then move on. It is essential to our mental, moral, and spiritual survival. A storm moves in whether mild or violent, makes its presence known, and then it passes. It is what it is.

I found myself in a seemingly impossible and difficult situation. I had five beautiful children to raise, an active career to maintain, and spiritual and mental mending to promote. I look back on this time of my life and wonder if I would have the strength to do now what I did then. The answer is always the same. If I keep strong in my faith and close to my Heavenly Father, He will provide the strength that I need to accomplish weathering whatever storm hits.

Though the days after my divorce were painful, hard, and depressing, I was able to find strength through faith and family to move forward. We still had family home evening, read our scriptures together, had family prayer, and attended our meetings. Does that mean the storm's aftereffects were mild or eased? No. It meant that I gained peace and understanding by the actions I took with my family. Those decisions gave me the energy, desire, and sheer guts to go forward with a positive attitude. I still had days where I was deeply depressed and exhausted from all my responsibilities, but as long as I was trying my best to keep the commandments, I seemed to find another day to which to look forward. I learned to channel energy from my anger and hurt into completing projects, rather than letting it defeat me physically, emotionally, and spiritually. I could not have done it alone. My Savior was walking by my side during the entire journey because I asked it of Him.

Family traditions were still maintained: Lake Powell vacations, Christmas, extravagant birthdays, chocolate chip cookies, and many more. It was a huge challenge and sometimes a roadblock when I had to explain to my young children the why that naturally came up. I taught them to hate the sin, not the sinner. I encouraged them to strive to have a good relationship with their father. It is hard to watch your children struggle with hurt and anger, but it is comforting to know that the same Spirit who guides and directs parents as individuals can enable the same parents to guide and direct their children. Again, this is not accomplished as a "lone wolf." It starts with a deep desire to do what is right and forged with the fire of love for God and family

I watched my children go through their individual storms. They were shunned by some because of our broken home. They lost the friendship of schoolmates. They had to divide their time up with the visitation schedules that were imposed on them by no action or doing of their own. My sons struggled through Scouts with no father to direct them. The priesthood was missed in our home. But my children were strong. They had been given a strong heritage and legacy from grandparents and others. Their lives evolved and my life grew and moved forward with hope. Sometimes it is what it is, and you just have to do what you can and make the best of it.

I have always been a social person and loved people, but after my divorce I was so busy working and raising my children, and dealing with financial burdens and lawyer and court costs that I hardly had any time for myself. I really didn't make time for myself. I felt that if I immersed myself completely in work and family I wouldn't have to deal with life as it was. Every once in a while I would get a babysitter and go to a movie or go golfing by myself. It was okay, but my heart yearned for the companionship I once had in marriage. I never said anything, but my unhappiness showed in my face and countenance. Children are very astute to pick up on these things, as were mine. The older ones suggested that I start dating again. At first that idea was out of the question. I simply did not want to date at all. They were persistent and pushy. Eventually I agreed to try. I became involved in an LDS dating site and ventured off on a few dates. I hated it. It was awkward and uncomfortable. I was about to give it up when I met a gentle, kind man who wasn't trying to prove anything and just wanted to be my friend.

We developed an unusually different relationship. It was a mature, kind, and loving relationship born from similar circumstances, goals, desires, and needs. He loved me for who I was at that moment in time, and he accepted and loved my children. I loved him in a different way than I had loved before. I respected him, because he was so selfless and God-fearing. Our interests were opposite and tastes different, but we were drawn to each other. Both of us had major trust issues to work through, but we managed to help each other and give the support that was needed to have our relationship grow. He asked each of my children for their permission to marry me, which made me love him even more. Eventually we were married and sealed in the Logan, Utah, Temple. My thoughts would frequently go back to the visions I had received about holding on to my temple blessings, and I knew that he was an answer to a prayer.

During our courting time, I kept having feelings and visions of a little boy. He would come to me and say, "Mommy, don't forget about me." I really struggled with this information because I was not married at the time and felt I might never be, and I was older in years. I actually questioned my sanity. But after my husband and I were married, the Spirit spoke so strongly to both of us that we made this subject part of our prayers and fasting. We both had a confirmation that we should have another child.

After a checkup from the doctor and the confirmation we received, we began our pursuit. A year and a half after we were married, my youngest son was born and welcomed into our family. He had five brothers and sisters that doted over him continually. To this day they all lay claims on raising him. The dreams I had experienced about him before he was born were made even more apparent by an experience I had.

Before he was born, I told my family about the dreams, so for Mother's Day they bought me a book. It was stories mothers had written that involved seeing their children before they were born. I read the book several times and then placed it on my book shelf. When my youngest son began to walk, he would go to that book shelf and pull that book off of the shelf. It was just the right height for him to reach. He would pull only that one off, no others. One night when I was putting him to bed, he asked me why I didn't wear my white night gown. I told him I didn't have a white night gown. He forcefully insisted that I did, because he said he remembered seeing me in it. I concluded that he had seen me in the temple in my white dress before he was born. That was the time he spoke to me and asked me not to forget him. This child has blessed our lives and definitely was supposed to be part of our family.

We experienced many ups and downs, detours, and setbacks in the years to follow. Only those who have faced trying to blend a family can deeply relate to this scenario. The same issues come up in most families; they are just approached a little more uniquely. The process of parenting takes on a whole new perspective. What surfaces are "your parenting methods," "my parenting methods," and "our parenting methods." You must put God first with all of these approaches, pray often, trust and love one another, and compromise. It takes time, patience, and practice to reach a win-win situation. We tried and failed and tried again and again, always getting up and putting one foot in front of the other. Storms and conflict came on a weekly basis at first, but then gradually subsided as we settled into forming a forever family centered on Christ and unconditional love. It was not perfect by a long shot, but intact, healthy, and growing together.

Every parent who loves their children deeply prays for their safety and protection from evil. That loving parent would rather suffer than see their child suffer. I was certainly no different. As much as I tried to ease the pain of divorce for my children, some of those storms just came. I learned that some of the storms that they endured had nothing to do with the divorce or was not affected by my righteous or unrighteous living. They just happened as part of life. My children needed to be tested and then grow and learn from those storms and progress in their own unique journey. They must learn to navigate their lives and use their free agency wisely. We as parents can only love them unconditionally, support their successes, and buoy them up when they start to sink. It is what it is. All you can do is your best.

Many of us go through more trials than others. At least it appears to be that way from our limited perspective. My middle son is one of those people. He was born with common childhood difficulties such as reflux and colic, and when he was ten months old he contracted parasites from irrigation water. I was unaware of it because it happened at a babysitter's home while I was at work. I observed my child getting more ill by the day. He wouldn't eat, he did not cut his teeth when he should have, and he did not gain any weight in an entire year. I had him in and out of the doctor's office and tried everything my pediatric nursing experience had taught me. In desperation I contacted a colleague I had worked with at the children's hospital in Salt Lake City. Pleading and tearful, I poured out my heart to him with the hope that he could help my child. We consequently embarked on a long painful journey of tests and hospitalizations. They ruled out cancer, cystic fibrosis, tumors, and other digestive disorders, and then they found the parasites. He was treated for them but left the hospital with feeding tubes and a feeding pack that ran twenty-four hours a day. It was hooked up to an IV pole. He was two years old. He became confined, but with this treatment he did progress to getting well. If this illness wasn't enough, his father, my ex-husband, rejected him. He denied him the love and companionship that a boy needs so much. It tore my heart out to watch.

My son grew and became a great athlete. He started playing basketball as a child. He was five years old when his father and I divorced. But in spite of the challenges he faced at a young age, he excelled in every way. He had two big desires: one to play in the NBA, and two to serve an LDS mission.

His bedroom walls were full of two things. Three walls were full of pictures of the Savior, most of those being large paintings that he had received as a Christmas or birthday gift. One wall had posters and autographed pictures of NBA stars that he admired. He slept with his special leather basketball.

His goals remained constant as he matured to becoming a teenager in high school. As he approached his junior year, preparations became intense for trying out for the basketball team, but a storm like no other blew his way. He began to lose his vision. We took him to an eye doctor, and my son was diagnosed with an eye disease that affects the cornea. Left untreated he would eventually become blind. His depth perception became distorted, and he struggled with seeing. He could not play basketball, golf, or even see to do his schoolwork well. Eventually he was put on the cornea transplant list as a last resort. The previous treatments had failed.

He put in his papers to serve a mission, but was denied because of his vision problems. He became depressed and unbelievably disappointed. His two dreams were destroyed. This storm was severe, yet I marveled how my son navigated his way through it. He focused on influencing a few inactive friends to go on full-time missions. He remained positive and close to his Heavenly Father.

Moving forward he applied for college, where he received help from government services for supplies so he could see his schoolwork. Eventually he received his first cornea transplant, which was successful. Still at the university, he continued to pursue his education. While there he faithfully served as a Church Service Missionary for the Church of Jesus Christ of Latter-Day Saints. The storm was not over, however. He started to lose the vision in his other eye and went back on the transplant list again. Months later he received a cornea, a sacred gift that was received from a relative. The relative, a young father, had been struck by a car and killed. He had put down his wishes to be an organ donor, and the family requested that the donation go to my son. This bittersweet situation made him strong and grateful. The Lord's tender mercies were showered upon him.

After a period of time he completely healed from his transplant. His branch president approached him and asked that he put in his papers again to serve a full-time mission. Reluctantly he agreed, because he was fearing the disappointment of denial. My son was nearing the age of twenty-four years old, which was closing in on the age limit of serving a full-time mission for young men. But after prayer, the papers were submitted. Unexplainable joy came when he received his call to serve a mission for the church in Louisville, Kentucky, Spanish speaking. His patience and faith were his strongholds that brought him to this point in his life. He had overcome so much and had remained faithful. The Lord had a purpose for my son to fulfill in a very special way. It would not be easy, and only he could accomplish it.

When my son's vision was first taken from him, the Lord blessed and compensated him with remarkable talent. As a young teen he was strongly encouraged to learn to play the piano. He took lessons because he was an obedient child, but he would have been happier to be outside playing basketball, so he never played well or learned to read music. One afternoon, while I was downstairs doing laundry, I heard the piano being played. It was beautiful music touched by eloquence. When I ventured upstairs to see who was playing, I could hardly catch my breath when I caught a glimpse of my son playing like he was an accomplished pianist. I inquired of him to find out where this new talent came from, and he could only say, "I don't know, Mom. I just sat down and started playing." The Lord had gifted him with extraordinary talent. This talent was put to many uses later in college and on his mission. He played several self-composed hymns in a medley at his zone conference that inspired all that attended.

His mission was spent in service and his mission president reported to me that my son had accomplished more in six months than most missionaries did in two years. On this same call his mission president told me that my son had been hit by a car and was in the hospital. He had lost his vision and was being treated. Oh, how my heart sank! I knew how he had wanted, prayed, and worked to get on that mission and how dedicated he was to being there. I felt his pain but was feeling helpless. Several calls from his mission president came and updates from the doctor. His vision loss was the result of something that didn't involve his transplants, but the doctors felt he should come back home to the doctors in Salt Lake City to be treated further.

Watching my son come down the ramp from the plane with tears rolling down his cheeks was one of the most painful experiences of my life. I had hoped my loving embrace would make his storm go away, but it did not. Time finally healed, faith replaced questionable doubts, and this storm blew over. Faith was challenged, questions erupted, anger spewed, and tears were shed. Normality seemed unreachable for a long time. "It is what it is." My son did his very best and came out a champion.

What makes a difference in the outcome of surviving a storm is the intense level of our trust and love of God. My son stayed focused on the big picture. Our family "ship" had been built strong, and the unconditional love he experienced from family and God had buoyed him up in his times of need. He now was experiencing the successes of his journey and was able to move forward blown by the winds of faith, endurance, and hope.

Recognizing a situation for what it is and then dealing with it the best you can, in my opinion, is a definition of life. My middle son had an extraordinary storm trauma hit him in his youth, and he is only one example. Every one of my children has had challenges, tests, and up-sets and has experienced pain, heartache, and suffering. As a mother I wanted to spare them from it, protect them, and shield them from the harsh rays of the atomic blasts that they felt. But we all understand that is impossible because "it is what it is."

Before I met my husband, I was experiencing the ups and downs of single parenthood, the exhaustion that never ends, the dilemma of being forced to have split personalities—one of mother and one of father, and the compounded financial worries that naturally fall into place with this particular role. Each one of my children had needs and wanted my attention. Some days I didn't know from where the energy would come. Even after I met and married my husband, the challenges still continued. Children resist blended families. Parents need a professional degree in "real-life" drama to master this chal-lenge. But again, the Lord has given us the tools to accomplish any task that is put to us. We just have to go to the hardware store and take action. In Isaiah 25:4, it speaks of what the Savior offers us as care and protection: "For thou hast been a strength to the poor, a strength to the needy in his distress, a refuge from the storm, a shadow from the heat, when the blast of the terrible ones is as a storm against the wall." Providing refuge is to provide comfort. What more do we need at our times of distress? It is what it is.

Not everything is a tragedy. I recall one year we were at Lake Powell in Utah. We went there every year until my parents passed away. My parents bought a boat for the whole family to use and to establish memories with their children and grandchildren. They generously sponsored a week-long stay at Lake Powell for my sister, my children, and me. It was the only vacation I could afford, and it became a blessing. It included my husband and our son later. One year, after a day of boating and skiing, we sensed a storm approaching. Storms and bad weather arise with flash-like quickness at Lake Powell. When you see or sense a storm, you have to seek shelter and anchor down immediately. We proceeded to do just that. The wind gained in intensity and the waves seemed to swell every few feet. The boat hammered against the walls of water and jumped the waves, becoming airborne for a few seconds. We were all experiencing strong anxiety and were hanging on to the railings of the boat with white knuckles. Life jackets were on and we were safe, but we were desperately trying to find shelter. Spotting a small cove in the distance, my father gave the boat a full throttle. We reached the shore and anchored down. By this time the wind was so strong we could hardly hear anyone speak. We frantically began securely putting the top and vinyl sides on the boat as we prepared for the storm. We were completely secured as the sun began going down. Everyone who had been anchoring the boat climbed in, and we all took deep breaths and exhaled sighs of relief. Thunder and lightning broke the peaceful relief that we were feeling. The sounds were magnified bouncing off the steep red-rock canyon walls. It was terrifying.

The situation was there, in its realism and splendor. Out came a large bag of strawberry twists licorice and cold bottles of water. To combat the boredom we played charades, and then my oldest son tried, and I state that lightly, to braid his sister's hair. He had never braided before, but it created some lighthearted laughter and passed the time while the storm raged. It is what it is. We assessed the situation, did the best we could, and then moved on.

You know, sometimes, you have the strength and the faith to weather a storm. You are able to recognize it for what it is, evaluate and dissect it, and you even dance in the rain that it produces. But don't you just sometimes want the rain to quit? I know I did. After navigating through storm after storm, I became weary. Don't get me wrong. I actually appreciate my trials because I have been truly blessed and have learned about the treasures of the lessons learned from them. Storms have a way, at times, to leave markings and carve out scars. After all, that is how canyons are formed. We just need to take the time to appreciate the beauty that has evolved and the splendor of what is right before us, which takes time and patience.

I raised my children in a beautiful home that had plenty of bedrooms, bathrooms, and storage. It was a lot to clean and maintain, but it met our needs. I had invested a great deal in our home. I worked three jobs to keep it after my divorce. My oldest daughter had her wedding reception in our backyard. Layers upon layers of memories existed within its walls. I remember birthday parties, sleepovers, backyard campouts, and barbeques. It was a second home to many of my children's friends. Teenagers gathered there for chocolate chip cookies after the high school games. They helped themselves to a giant jar of M&M's that sat by my back door and was filled periodically with colored candy to match the season.

Nights by the fire included family home evenings, scripture study, games, laughter, and lots and lots of love. Food was cooked, baked, eaten, and canned in a frantically busy kitchen. Sprinklers were fun to run through as a pastime in the hot summer months. Two wonderful blue spruce pines were planted in front and grew with my children. The pines were both decorated with tiny white Christmas lights during the holidays. Pets were raised with love and care. Kiki, our dog, was buried on the property. She used to eat my strawberries from my strawberry patch when they were ripe. One time she was sprayed by a skunk. We put out the tiny blow-up swimming pool and bathed her in tomato juice to get the stench out of her fur. She became ill and had to be hospitalized. The children gave up their vacation money to see that she got the care that she needed. Pictures of family members adorned the walls of this home, and it had a special feeling when you entered. We were there for thirty years.

I had been struggling at my work with department changes and my husband was struggling with layoffs. The housing market was crashing and the economy was sickened with problems. We both lost our jobs. Besides working with the banks, we also took money out of our savings and retirement to help our situation. We consulted our church leaders and even involved a lawyer, but to no avail. The government illegally seized our home, and we lost everything. The bank reprocessed my husband's vehicle, we had no employment, our savings were gone, and we were edging into our sixties. This storm I truly did not comprehend. I could not see any reason why I should be positive or count my blessings in the wake of this adversity. I was devastated. Hurt, anger, resentment, confusion, fear, and panic—oh, yeah, they were all present and accounted for.

I had three garage sales. We had to get storage sheds to house some of our belongings. You accumulate a lot over thirty years. Family again came to the rescue as much as possible. Hours and days were spent on a borrowed computer to find us a place to live. I went into mourning. It was a huge loss to my family and me. I could see that it was just a building and I still had my family, but the significance of the loss was substantial and the damage from this storm irreparable. Sadly, it is what it is.

Okay, now what? Nothing I did changed my situation. I did not get my home back. Moving on was painful. We found a rental home that we quickly moved into, and I started making it personalized. It was nice and comfortable, but still didn't feel like home. My husband and I both, eventually, became employed again, but not without considerable sacrifice. To get back on our feet financially, my husband went to work in the oil fields of North Dakota. He came home for five days every three weeks. It was irritating and difficult to do, and our family struggled. I tried hard to stay focused and not lose my view of the whole picture while telling myself that I could do it for five years and things would get better. There were times I doubted, times I cried, times of exhaustion, and times of fear. I kept hearing my mother's words, "count your blessings" and "you can do this, Debi." They gave me a lot of comfort. I missed her.

Satan wants us to lose hope, be discouraged, give up, and have fear. That way he can control us and our destiny. At this point in my life, I had been strategically prepared to face astronomical storms, categories seven and eight! I wasn't about to give in to any of the nonsense that Satan had in store. We ended up moving again, went through a couple of job losses, and still survived. I fell and had to have surgery in the middle of the move. I received help from ward members, family members, and friends. Support came from my husband from a distance. My dance in the rain is slowing down because I'm older, but it is definitely still there. After all, it is what it is.

For Cryin' Out Loud

WE EACH HAVE a phrase, word, or saying that is uttered from our mouths when we want to express pure disbelief or shock. A myriad of them exists, derived from family background, education, religion, demographic location, and culture. A few that I recall are "What?" "Are you kidding me?" "That's just great!" "Oh, brother!" "Whatever." "You're joking, right?" "Oh, wow!" "Oh, my gosh!" "What the heck?" and one of my favorites, "For cryin' out loud!" My mother uniquely added "in the basement" to "for cryin' out loud." Thus it became, "For cryin' out loud in the basement." Personally I never understood what the basement had to do with anything, but that's how I remember it. Sometimes these expressions are uttered when we don't know what else to say. A few of them are not the best choices, but they are part of our vocabulary. Over a lifetime, no matter how short or well-lived that lifetime is, we all can relate to the earth-shaking shock of traumatic events. Storms hit all of us. Some of those storms are close and some are a bit more distant. We may watch or observe others go through raging storms that cause our compassion to stir and emotions to surface. Louisa May Alcott said, "Painful as it may be, a significant emotional event can be the catalyst for choosing a direction that serves us—and those around us—more effectively." Have you ever been faced with a choice that changed your course and affected all those around you? A choice that was made because of a significant, traumatic event that you experienced or observed?

I recall one of the most significant choices I made was in high school. I was enrolled in seminary, and we had been studying the atonement, repentance, and forgiveness. I was a typical teenager and paid attention to about half of the lessons. I was also searching to find my own testimony by asking questions of myself like, "Why do I believe this?" or "Will this concept or doctrine help me be a better person?" Dating had become an intricate part of my itinerary, and hormones were clashing with the concept of making good choices. I had made some mistakes and wanted desperately to know I could repent and be forgiven, so when my seminary class talked about repentance, I paid close attention. The instructor had made an impact on my perception of evil and how Satan would do anything to keep me from following the path of the Savior.

With that in mind, I decided one night to ask the Lord to help me find a testimony of repentance so I would have a desire to embrace that doctrine and get right with God. It was late when I finally prepared for sleep. The ritual was the same each evening: shower, brush teeth, say prayers. Usually I closed my drapes in my bedroom. One large window was located on each of two walls of the room. My bed rested underneath one of those windows. This night the moon was full and hung in the sky like an oversized searchlight. I loved having the moonlight shine in my room, so I left the drapes open. I was positioned in bed so I could see the bedroom door which led to the hallway, and two closets—one double closet with sliding wooden doors located on the left of my bed and one tucked in the opposite corner. It was a single closet with a grey collapsible vinyl door. The hallway was dark and everyone was already asleep when I finished my prayers. It was daylight bright in my room, and I remember thinking how beautiful it was as I was getting ready to close my eyes.

I glanced over toward the grey closet, and my heart almost stopped. It seemed everything was in slow motion, as it happened over the course of a few minutes. I cautiously and slowly turned my head in that direction. My eyes widened as I saw a dark figure that stood by the grey closet. It was a generic figure with no face. It turned its head toward me, and I felt its gaze, even though it had no eyes. Immediately the air became freezer cold and a dark mist filled the entire room. A heaviness came over me, and it was like someone was sitting on me, smothering me, so I couldn't breathe. I wanted to cry. I could not. I wanted to scream and opened my mouth to make an effort. I could not. I wanted to call out to my dad in the next room to evoke his priesthood powers, but no sound emerged. Picking up on the sound of my heart pounding, my breathing became more rapid. I was terrified. I recognized this figure as pure evil, one of Satan's servants. In my mind, I started repeating the words of my seminary teacher who had told us that we had the power over Satan; we just had to call on the Savior. Pleading with my Savior, I asked Him to rebuke this evil. I repeated my efforts several times.

I awoke the next morning exhausted. I got ready for school and didn't really recall the previous night until I arrived home that after-noon. I told my mother and father about my experience and then shared it with my stake president. I related to him how I studied and prayed about repentance in a desire to gain a testimony of my own. He told me that I made righteous choices and because of my deep de-sire to gain knowledge and a testimony, Satan was trying to stop me. Receiving counsel and a priesthood blessing from my stake president gave me the courage to continue my pursuit. I didn't realize at this time in my life that my decision to serve the Lord and gain my own testimony would vastly affect those friends and family members that I held dear to my heart and my future children and grandchildren. This was an "Oh, wow!" experience.

After graduation I attended Utah State University in Logan, Utah. I had received a performing arts scholarship and was pursuing my dreams. Music theory, choir, piano classes, and general education classes filled my days. Playing my guitar and writing songs were my pastimes and served as great stress relievers. One afternoon I was sit-ting in the Commons. It was in between classes, and I was immerged in writing a new song on my guitar. My aspiration was to be the next country music star and have my music published. Really! Inspiration was flooding through my thoughts as I wrote the words down on a piece of paper. I stopped periodically and picked up my guitar to strum out a tune to match the words. Annoyingly I was interrupted when I heard a voice call my name, and I turned to see who it was. No one was there. I shook it off and dismissed it. I again heard distinctly the voice saying, "This is not the right career for you. You could never support a family, and it is a bad environment." I immediately said one of those sayings, "What the heck?" out loud. I felt kind of foolish. This experience kept tormenting me, and I couldn't get it out of my mind. I would think about it all day and dream about it at night. I felt the promptings of the Spirit so strongly that I simply could not ignore them.

After a lot of prayer and literally arguing with the Spirit, I made another ardent decision in my life. I dropped out of that school, changed my major, and transferred to the University of Utah, where I pursued a degree in nursing. I gave up my scholarship and had to rely on various means of financial support to attend the university. I put my whole trust in the Lord because I knew this was what He wanted me to do. For the life of me I couldn't understand why, because science was not my strongest subject in school, but my trust in Him would direct my life later and help me stay my course through the rough storms ahead. Here was an "Are you kidding me?" moment that I would understand only later in my life.

University life was challenging. I made good decisions. I made bad decisions. One choice that I made was to stay focused on who I was and the gospel. I reminded myself often to hold fast to my inherent values while living an exciting social life. A calling I received in my branch humbled me and helped me keep things in perspective. I was called to teach the Gospel Doctrine class, a class that was usually taught by returned missionaries on campus.

My feelings of inadequacy and doubting my capabilities gave in to Satan's influence on my progress. I accepted the calling because I didn't dare say no, but I was not overjoyed about it. Hours and hours were spent in preparation. I studied the scriptures more than I ever had and spent a substantial amount of time on my knees. I let peoples' opinion about me get in the way of teaching with the Spirit.

I was so scared of what the class thought that I engaged in self-sabotaging. The class consisted of intelligent, mature individuals with a balance of women, returned missionaries, and professional students. Occasionally a visitor would come in, but wouldn't say much.

A young man began gracing the classroom quite often. He was well-dressed, respectful, and had a Middle Eastern accent. I let his presence intimidate me without even having a conversation with him. I judged him, and I regretted it later. On occasion he would interrupt me to ask deep questions, and often I did not have the answer for him. I would get embarrassed when I couldn't spar with him about religious theology. Finally out of frustration one day, I made another decision that would affect the class and this young man. I made this decision because he asked me to prove that what I was teaching was true. I felt the Spirit prompt me to be upfront and honest with him. I told him that I couldn't prove it in a factual or scientific way, but I knew it to be true because the Spirit had testified to me that it was indeed true, and I felt it and knew it with all my being.

I was glad when the trimester was over and I could head home for Christmas break. While home I received a phone call. I asked who it was, and my mom said, "I don't know; he wouldn't give his name." After I cautiously said hello, I was greeted by a voice with the same recognizable accent from the Gospel Doctrine class. He reminded me of who he was and refreshed my memory of the questions he had asked me in class and the testimony I had born to him. Great news followed as he announced that he had been baptized over Christmas, and he thanked me for the influence I had on him in making that decision. "Oh, my gosh!" That was amazing!

We often don't realize the magnitude of the decisions that we make. We can't see the multitudes of rippling influences that meet their paths. The results and consequences sneak up on us, and we are shocked and surprised. We find ourselves surrounded with "Wow!" "Are you kidding me?" "Oh, my gosh!" or just no words at all. These are the times that our ship is sailing smooth waters, the skies are promising calm, and the breezes are cool and comforting. These are times when we step back and really become grateful for our blessings and the life we have. We dance in the rain with a smile on our face knowing that there is growth, progress, and rainbows in the future. It might be a rainbow reflecting off a very small mud puddle, but it is still a rainbow—a promise of hope.

One of the best decisions I made in my life was to become a nurse. That career choice has blessed my life on more than one occasion. The main reason I chose nursing was because of prodding by the Spirit; but I also wanted to help people and make a difference. I decided early in my career that I wanted to be a compassionate, effective, and caring nurse. Studying hard became a regular scene, because I took my career choice seriously. It wasn't just about getting good grades, but it became a passion to truly understand my skills and be proficient at delivering quality care to my patients. This part of my life gave much more to me than I felt I gave to it. Nursing became my anchor financially to be able to support a family and maintain a household.

My first job as a Registered Nurse was at Primary Children's Hospital in Salt Lake City. I truly loved this hospital and the individuals that gave of their time and skills. Magnificent life lessons were learned and many storms experienced, both personally and through patients and their families. While working in surgery, I observed the families of the patients that were going to have surgery, particularly the mother. The procedures varied from simply having tubes put in the ears to brain surgery or open-heart surgery. All these procedures had a commonality: mothers worried the same. Their concerns were real and heartfelt, no matter the intensity or difficulty of the procedure being performed. It taught me to be acutely aware and sensitive to all individuals' perception of their problems. No matter how small my perception might be, their perception was what really mattered. I think this helped me to realize that Heavenly Father wants to hear about our concerns, no matter how small we might think they are. He loves us, and our fears and concerns are important to Him.

The children at this hospital taught me much more than I ever taught them. I had just received report on the patients that I would be caring for one afternoon. I grabbed my light-blue stethoscope, looped it around my neck, and scooped up a clipboard with a pen attached. Computers were nonexistent in the rooms for charting. Everything was done by hand on paper. My colleagues had given me a brief description of the little girl that I was about to see. She was four years old and had been hospitalized for complications from the chicken pox. I just needed to get her vital signs, which consisted of temperature, heart rate, lung sounds, and blood pressure. This exam was so routine to me that I didn't prepare myself adequately for the following encounter.

The door to her room was closed, so I knocked softly and asked to enter. A sweet, high-pitched voice said, "Sure! Come on in!" As I entered her room, my eyes became fixed on her hospital bed. The bed was cranked to a sitting position and an oversized pillow cradled her back. Long, curly, dark hair fell forward over part of her face, and she shook her head to direct it out of her eyes. She looked up and grinned. This beautiful child had been without arms since birth. From the bottom of her hospital gown extended two healthy pink legs. Her right leg was curled inward and her petite foot had a skinny crayon tucked between the great and second toe. The left foot was being used to secure the piece of paper on which she was creating her artwork.

When I entered she immediately asked my name and then introduced herself. Usually that is what I do when I enter a patient's room. She beamed as she told me about her artwork and made it clear that it was for me. A young father was in the room and lovingly watched his daughter's independence blossom. I was then given instructions, by my four-year-old friend, on protocol. I was to treat her as anyone else, not differently. She explained that she had to do her chores at home just like her brother and sister, and they were treated equally. A determined "Don't feel sorry for me" followed with a confirmation from Dad that she was correctly directing the conversation.

I eventually was able to take her vital signs and bid her goodbye. Quietly and softly I closed her door, making sure the last thing she saw was the smile on my face. When I knew I was alone, I bowed my head, and with tears running down my cheeks, I thanked God for the opportunity I had to meet this extraordinary child. I vowed on that day that I would strive to have the kind of positive-driven attitude that she had and try my best to handle the storms that came at me like she had in her example. Shaking my head and drying my tears, I definitely thought to myself, "Are you kidding me?"

I had many encounters with brave children at that hospital. As I started having a family of my own, it became increasingly difficult to travel and work there, so my career took a detour. I made the decision to work one or two days a week so I could spend more time at home. I did staff nursing for a couple of agencies in the Salt Lake Valley. My experiences varied from working in the burn unit at the University of Utah Hospital to medical/surgical floors and ICU's. I was asked if I would consider doing a private-nursing-care job at a local hospital. The agency went into detail about this particular assignment and explained why it was so difficult. I hesitated because they said if I declined, they would understand. I wondered, what could be so bad? I accepted the assignment.

When I arrived I was given report from the staff. I was shocked to hear how negatively they felt about the patient. The staff warned that she was very demanding and unreasonable. They left me with the words, "I'm glad it's you taking care of her and not me." This patient was an unmeasurably wealthy and influential person and was staying in a VIP room. Her family had deep history in the community and made innumerable contributions to it. She was used to being waited on and fussed over. Many individuals were under her household employment. Giving orders were second nature to her. When I entered her room, I respectfully introduced myself to her and was greeted with, "I hope you last longer than the others."

The first few weeks were a real struggle for me. I had to remind myself every minute I was with her that she was very ill and dying and I needed to be compassionate. She criticized everything I did, from procedures to fluffing her pillow. I decided early that no matter what she said to me I was not going to let her get to me, and I was going to give her the best care I could. Gradually she softened. I believe it was because of a particular dining incident that occurred.

She was irritated and unhappy when her meals were served to her on hospital plates and set on a hospital tray. She had previously asked the hospital staff to serve her meals on a table with a linen tablecloth and the food served on her china. Of course they refused. I made a determined decision one afternoon to make it happen for her. She was dying, and besides, her family had probably paid for the whole wing where she was staying.

I spoke with the staff and made arrangements for a small table to be brought to her room. I told them I would handle everything so as to not disturb their duties or schedule. I then called and made arrangements to get her china, silverware, and linen cloth brought to the room. With her direction, I set the table and ordered her food from the kitchen. I met the nursing staff in the hallway and transferred the food to her china. When she sat down for dinner, a transformation came over her. She sat straight up, even though it was painful for her, and an aura of dignity surrounded her. She schooled me on the "properness" involved in serving tea and opened up and began telling me about her family and stories of her travels. It was the start of a wonderful relationship.

Weeks passed, and she became weaker. She would always ask about her husband and grandchildren. She didn't get many visitors, which broke my heart. Here was a stately woman who by all appearances seemed to have everything. She had lived a life of luxury and adventure, but in her time of need, money and prestige did not replace family. She held fast to our time spent together and took advantage of that time to tell me about her religion, the awards she had received, famous people she had met, and what her greatest fears were. I was privileged to meet her cook, butler, and company CEO's.

She received one visit from her family. It was on her husband's birthday. The company had given him a new car as a gift. The conversation consisted of what he was going to do with the car because he was wheelchair bound and couldn't drive. He decided that he was going to give it to his driver. And that was the extent of the visit.

As it became apparent that she did not have much time left on this earth, she clung to her material wealth. She insisted that I order her furs to be sent to the hospital room so she could wear them. She began giving things away. When she discovered that my daughters loved to dance, she provided tickets to see *The Nutcracker*. Stubbornly she would not take no for an answer. One afternoon she grabbed my hand and pulled me close. "You're the nicest Catholic girl I know." I lovingly explained to her that I was not Catholic, but I was a member of the Church of Jesus Christ of Latter-Day Saints. She was okay with that parcel of information.

One night after I had given her the medications that she needed and prepared her for sleep, she asked me to come and sit by her side next to her bed. The walls of the room were painted in rich fall colors and the furniture was ornate, walnut wood with velvet pads on the chairs. A small brass lamp sat in the middle of the table by the window. Drapes were closed to promote a more restful sleep. Beautiful, massive paintings hung on the wall, and the light switch covers were gold. Her hospital room resembled a hotel suite.

That night stillness lurked and the quiet made me feel as if I was somewhere almost sacred. Again she took my hand. She asked me if I believed in heaven and if I knew what happened after death. I shared my deepest feelings about the hereafter and my testimony of life eternal. I asked her if she was afraid, and her response was, not surprisingly, "Yes." She asked me to stay with her. I clasped her frail, weak hand and watched her sigh and stare at the ceiling. I reminded her that she was loved. The silence was heavy as she drifted into a deep, unreturnable sleep.

How could a beautiful person such as that one have so much in life and yet die alone? I gained much respect for her. She taught me a lot in her own quirky way. I learned to appreciate family, that it is a treasure, unmeasurable and irreplaceable. I only wish she could have had hers. "What the heck?"

Eventually I turned my nursing career back to my specialty, pediatrics. I became the case manager for approximately sixty pediatric patients. Some of the young individuals had cancer. The storms they faced were heart-wrenching. My faith was challenged many times as I witnessed one child after another suffer with pain and illness. At times I wasn't sure I knew why these children had to suffer, and I took my concerns to the Lord often. Once in a while I would get a patient that I followed for an extended period of time—sometimes years. I became unusually close to them and to their families. A collage of pictures and drawings adorned my desk, along with sporadic thank-you cards and invitations to Make-A-Wish events. That time of my life was hard but rewarding.

One particular family I simply cannot forget. Family dynamics consisted of Mom, Dad, two boys, and one girl. Before I came on the scene, the little girl was diagnosed with cancer and received chemotherapy. Treatment was unsuccessful, and she passed away at a young age. One year after she died, the youngest boy was diagnosed with the same cancer. He immediately began chemotherapy. I would go to their home to administer his chemo. He was only five years old. Even though he was sick and nauseated most of the time, he managed to have a big grin and an infectious giggle when I was there. He taught me how to play video games. That's how he would spend his time during therapy. He was one of the bravest souls I have ever met. He endured painful IVs, chemotherapy, oral medications, and weekly blood draws, but rarely did he complain.

His illness started to destroy the family. Stress from catastrophic medical bills and the loss of his sister pulled his parents apart. They eventually divorced, and he and his mom and brother moved from their home to a more affordable apartment. He took a downhill spiral and became so ill that he was not expected to live. While barely surviving on palliative care, he seemed to hang on to something. I learned in my experience in pediatrics that children face death differently than most adults. They seem to need permission to pass. So it was with this young boy. Because he was bedridden and semicomatose, his mom was tortured by grief and worry. Dad was in denial and rejection mode. Older brother felt forgotten and dismissed.

It was two a.m., and I received a call from his mother. She pleaded with me to come. Her voice was quivering and desperate. When I arrived my little friend was on the couch. All IVs had been removed two days prior. Outside, Dad cried and paced in front of the house. In the bedroom Mom was sobbing into a pillow. A relative greeted me and quietly gave me updates on the situation. Her directions were muffled. I focused my eyes on the couch. My sweet friend lay on his back with pillows behind his head and shoulders. He had a crocheted comforter gently tucked around his body. The feeling in the room was surprisingly peaceful which was a contrast to this devastating event. A small lamp was on in the dining room that gave just enough light to the living room so I could see the details on the sleeping child's face. A look of concern was captured in his furrowed eyebrows.

I knelt down by the edge of the couch and took both his hands in mine. Talking quietly, I told him that I understood his reluctance to leave. I reaffirmed that his parents loved him very much and his brother loved him too. I explained that I knew how hard it must be for him, but that he need not worry about his family. They would be okay. Even though he was semicomatose, I believe he heard every word I said.

I rose up and went into the bedroom to console his mother. I embraced her as I explained that her son needed permission to pass on. Our conversation went back and forth validating feelings and answering questions. I reassured her that I would be by her side and that her son would hear her. We quietly approached her son. She knelt by his side and took his little face in her hands. As only a loving mother could, she beautifully expressed her love for him and comforted him with words of unconditional love, removing the guilt he might feel, and giving her permission for him to move on and pass through the veil of this life. She gently kissed his forehead and said goodbye. Hugging herself tightly and bowing her head, she retreated into the bedroom.

Approaching the dad was more difficult. He was crying uncontrollably and stating over and over how he couldn't go through it again. I gently put my hand on his shoulder and explained to him how his son was staying behind because he needed permission from his dad to leave. I told him how his son required his dad to gently guide him through this process and assure him that his family would be okay. After a few minutes the dad agreed to go talk to his son. Awkwardly he approached the couch, shrugged his shoulders, took a deep breath as he glanced back at me, and began talking to his son. Love flowed from this father as he carefully chose his words. He ruffled his son's thick, black hair as he said, "It's okay for you to go, but we will miss you." He then returned to the yard. I could hear his sobbing cries and a conversation that seemed to be directed at God.

Weighted down with emotion, I sat on the edge of the couch close to my little friend. I gently stroked his cheek and told him that it was okay to go. As I told him to go toward the light and look for his grandmother and sister, I observed peace blanket his brow, and it relaxed. He quietly took his last breath. "For cryin' out loud!

By living life, we all experience death. It is part of the journey. Sometimes we have questions that don't seem to have immediate answers or reasons that make any sense. I experienced a lot of death in my nursing career, and I also saw many miracles. I have never regretted the decision I made while at Utah State University in the Commons when I heard the promptings of the Spirit to redirect my life. That "Are you kidding me?" moment proved to be one of the most transforming decisions of my life. It's okay to question and explore answers. We all have unique lives that are individually tapered to our environment, culture, and experiences.

Charles M. Schulz, author of the "Peanuts" cartoon strip, posted a quote that came from the women of the series. The character Lucy said, "Today's woman needs more to fall back on than brains, brawn, and beauty." I strove for all of these character traits. But there is one essential trait that is missing in this quote: spirituality. Every storm that has ever come my way has hit with brutal force. I have been humbled many times by realizing that I can't rely on my own brains and brawn. I need God in all things. When you realize that you cannot journey through life on your own, that you can't sail your ship without guidance, that you cannot have true happiness without understanding your worth and purpose, then and only then do you truly find your way.

Our decisions should hinge on our Father's approval. We must use our agency wisely and cherish the gift and freedom that it affords us. We are in charge of much of our lives. We forge the direction our ship will sail by the decisions that we make each and every day. Given discernment, if we ask for it, we can step back and weigh our decisions carefully, pray about them sincerely, and bravely act on the guidance we receive. We will still have our "What?" moments, and we will possibly regret some of these choices, but trust in the Lord, for it is His "work and glory to bring to pass the eternal life of man." He wants us to succeed. He wants us to have joy. His influence will assist us in making righteous decisions that will benefit ourselves and those with whom we come in contact. Decide to dance in the rain that a storm may bring. However you orchestrate that dance is your choice. But make that choice, "for cryin' out loud!"

Everything Happens for a Reason

IN THE DOCTRINE and Covenants 88:42, it says, "And again, verily I say unto you, he hath given a law unto all things, by which they move in their times and their seasons." Everything happens for a reason. God planned it that way. We can spend a lifetime in frustration because we refuse to accept this God-given rule of the universe. We can expend all our energy trying to reason out the why's and how's of events. Or we can gain the wisdom of knowing how to function in the season we are in by living life to the fullest and doing the best we can. We will certainly question the purpose of certain events in our lives and become bewildered when we try to make sense of things. Heavenly Father knew that we would not be perfect, that we would make bad choices and enact terrible decisions. He carefully created the universe we live in and gave us very calculated guidelines to assist us in our journey. We need to recognize His hand in all things and accept that our time is not always His time. Our ship will sail a smoother journey, storms will be met with determined strength, houses and testimonies will stand firmer if we accept His planned course of action and allow Him to be the captain of our souls.

When something happens in your life that is either different from what you had planned or it blindsided you with harshness, you have a tendency to wonder, "What am I supposed to learn from this?" You ask, "Why?" over and over. You may become depressed and question your worth. This is exactly what the adversary wants. He wants you to become discouraged and give up. But don't! Everything that happens to you, no matter how small or insignificant it may seem, has a purpose, and there is a reason behind it. That reason may not be profound and hit like a lightning bolt; rather it may be a quiet "Ah-ha" moment. Nevertheless, it is there. Search for it. Pray to understand it. Don't give up!

An incident occurred when I was a teenager that made me feel like my world had been crushed. When I talk about it now, it seems really small and trite. But the feelings I had back then were huge and genuinely real.

In junior high I struggled with typical teenage problems, like most individuals. I cared deeply about what my friends and family thought about me. I wanted to be liked and feel accepted by my peers. Athletics and dancing came naturally to me, and I was fortunate enough to excel in those fields. I decided that I wanted to be a cheerleader. I began the pursuit years before I could actually try out. Training included dance and gymnastic lessons. My parents sacrificed for dance lessons but didn't have the money for gymnastic lessons. I knew that cheerleaders had to have gymnastic skills, so I sought help from friends and proceeded to become a self-taught gymnast.

The backyard at my house, the one with the sliding glass doors, was a massive blanket of soft, green grass. I spent hours every day doing cartwheels, backbends, and self-taught back handsprings. I couldn't get the back handspring down, so I improvised and changed it to a front handspring. When I did it right, it was pretty impressive. I did pushups and sit-ups to strengthen my arms and ran each night to gain strength in my legs. When I prepared to do a handspring in the backyard I began by focusing my stare on the ground. I took several deep breaths, clinched my fists, and ran like I was approaching a broad jump. I precisely placed both of my hands securely on the ground at running speed and pushed off high enough with my arms to allow myself to flip one rotation in the air and land on my feet. Most of the time I overshot the flip and landed on my face. Bruises and scratches covered my legs and arms. The soreness in my bones and muscles lingered and made me conscious of the irritating aches. This practice continued for three years. By the time I entered high school, that annoying handspring was perfected.

I tried out for drill team my sophomore year and made it. I wanted to get the dancing experience that drill team offered. I applied that experience to my cheerleading aspirations. Going to school early every day became a ritual. I was up by five a.m. and to school by six. Workouts were grueling. I starved myself to maintain my weight. I ran and worked on my gymnastic skills in my spare time. I maintained high grades, because academics was a priority. Attending seminary and church regularly gave me a satisfying balance in my life. My confidence grew, and I made a lot of diverse friends. I enjoyed people, so I never "hung out" with one particular crowd.

Approximately six hundred students comprised my high school student body. Six cheerleaders formed the varsity squad. Cheerleader selection and tryouts were a calculated process. First a pre-tryout was judged by the faculty. It consisted of skills demonstration, cheer ability, and dancing routines. Twelve girls, selected by the faculty, performed in front of the student body. The students voted for the top six, who became the cheerleading squad.

Before the faculty tryouts, I met with one of the current cheerleaders. She taught me several routines that I was required to perform. Perfecting jumps, kicks, and gymnastics skills were all part of the preparation. I met with an inspirational girl named Millie. Millie was two years older than me. Her infectious smile put everyone at ease. I immediately felt comfortable around her. I worked to the point of exhaustion. She complimented me on my style and told me how much she and the other cheerleaders wanted me to make the squad, which gave me hope.

Finally I made it through the faculty tryouts and was grouped with three others. We would perform and try out in front of the student body. Most of my friends were skilled and didn't need much help. Occasionally I was asked to give tips on either dancing or gymnastics.

We needed a certain grade point average to be eligible for tryouts. One of my friends coerced her teacher to change her grade so she could try out. Those who honestly worked hard were bitterly disappointed in her decision, but most of us just commented about it and then dismissed it.

During the week leading up to try outs, a mother of one of the girls who was trying out made a complaint about the actions of that particular girl. The girl was barred from tryouts. I really didn't think much about it until one day a boy approached me in the hall. He said he heard it was my mother who made the complaint. I reacted with a strong, "It was not." I was perplexed at his accusation, because I would never do such a thing. He continued, "I'm going to make sure that you don't make cheerleader."

I felt devastated and betrayed. The student body voted on who they wanted in the cheerleading squad. I was deeply concerned about the threat from this student.

The day of tryouts came, and I had so much adrenaline going through my body that I overworked some of my muscles. I took a muscle relaxer to help with the discomfort. I said a prayer. A bit of nausea settled in my stomach. I watched each one of my friends walk into the gymnasium and perform the routines they had learned. The bleachers were full of screaming, cheering students, and I noted where my closest friends were seated. I recalled the many "good-luck" greetings that I received earlier as I passed friends and acquaintances in the halls. A faint smile came over my face. I performed my routines with precision and enthusiasm. I ended the last routine and prepared to run out onto the gym floor to do my gymnastic stunts and raise the crowd's excitement. Just like I had practiced in the backyard, I kept thinking. I had done it a million times. Hitting the floor running, I placed my hands strategically in front of me and then felt my whole body spring up and forward. Suddenly I found myself face down, looking at the gym floor. It smelled of a mixture of wax and dust. My eyes were closed in disbelief. I picked myself up and did an awkward bow, laughed briefly, and continued with my jumps and cheers.

The votes from the student body were processed and counted during the remainder of the day and early evening. Results would be announced at a dance held later. I prepared myself before I went to the dance. I deserved to be a cheerleader and wanted it badly. I hoped I could accept whatever the results would be. It seemed like hours that I waited on the dance floor for the varsity cheerleaders to come to the mike and make the announcement. Friends bombarded me with a pat on my back and an "I voted for you" or "You've got this" called out as they passed by. One by one the names were announced. None included me. One girl selected could not do any gymnastics, forgot her routines, and cried in front of the whole student body. I was humiliated. How could this happen? I prepared for this for a very long time and I could not understand why I didn't deserve to have what I worked and sacrificed for. I left the dance in tears. It did not deter Millie. She stopped me on my way out. She choked back tears as she told me that the varsity cheerleaders could not believe that I didn't make it. They recounted the votes three times. I lost by only one vote.

I couldn't help but wonder at that time if the one vote came from the student who had made the false accusations against me. I felt betrayed. It hurt my heart and stung my pride. It wasn't enough at the time to entertain the "whys" and "what ifs" that kept lurking in my mind. I couldn't figure it out then; I needed more wisdom and maturity to be able to accept my circumstances and understand my purpose.

Everything happens for a reason, no matter how small or unimportant one might think it is. Lessons can be learned from even experiences like the one that I had in high school. Oh, it really affected me; don't get me wrong, but I learned to readjust my priorities. I found that I had just as many friends after the ordeal.

The experience of growing by learning self-discipline, hard work, and perseverance would prove to be an invaluable lesson. It may not seem like a big deal to most people, but becoming a cheerleader was a big deal to me. Not making cheerleader happened for a reason in my life. I had to learn to forgive the boy who fell to rumor and gossip. I learned to laugh at myself, pick myself up (literally), and move forward when faced with an embarrassment. Discovering that my character and integrity made up who I was, and what position I held did not, was a life-changing experience that I can look back on and appreciate. There is a time and season for everything.

I was taught at a young age to increase and share any talents that God saw fit to bestow upon me. I turned from my passion for cheerleading to my passion for music. I suffered through piano lessons at a young age. When I became proficient at the piano, I begged my mother to get me a guitar. I felt it was less structured and gave me the creative freedom that I craved. When I was growing up I was encouraged always to share my talent to help others. My first solo was at a church talent show where I was dressed as a young Snow White and sang, "I'm Wishing." When I was quite young I was asked to sing often in church, at community events and nursing homes. Choir and competitions became a deep-rooted part of who I was. Music shaped my life for good.

At a time of loss it is important to find a way to give to others and lift them up. This is Christ-like love called charity. I felt I could use my music to do that. Mark 8:35-36 states, "For whosoever will save his life shall lose it; but whosoever shall lose his life for my sake and the gospel's, the same shall save it." This magnificent principle is also found in the scriptures in Luke and Matthew.

No matter what your talent may be, if you share it to bless the lives of others, your talent will be magnified. I found this to be true in the different seasons of my life. After high school I embarked on a performing musical tour of Europe. It was chaperoned by the drama department head and several parents. I had this grand opportunity because my selfless, generous parents sacrificed monetarily so I could go. There is a time and season for everything. This was the season for me to grow and share my talent. My dad donated his snowmobile, which was sold at a raffle to get the needed funds for the trip. Mom and Dad sold other valuables too. The group would be gone for a month, and it would take a lot of raffle tickets.

I felt I was experiencing a dream come true. I was blessed. But I wanted to make sure that I did not misuse my talent and that I showed my gratitude to my parents, family, and God. The trip crept up on me, and before I had time to soak it in, I was on a huge plane. It seated four passengers on each side of the middle section, which seated six. We lifted into the air at Kennedy Airport in New York City. The massive airliner soared effortlessly into the black night leaving behind speckled lights on the ground. The Statue of Liberty faded in the background until eventually I could see only black, with the lights of the airplane illuminating our cabin. Twelve hours stretched out, and most of us slept. I was able to play my guitar, and groups gathered and sang familiar songs to help pass the time. There was a feeling of melancholy as I left my country. Everything happens for a reason. I was headed for an adventure that would enrich and change my life.

Greece was the starting point. I visited Corinth and walked where the Savior walked. I met many good and delightful people. I shared my music with them, which bridged any language barriers that were present. The vastness of my world began to unfold as I saw God's love in people who were different from me. Next came Italy, and my imagination exploded as I observed and visited the Colosseum and the Vatican. Art and history flooded my mind, and I was humbled by my blessings and privileges. I sang and played my guitar at a fountain a short distance from the Vatican. People smiled as if they understood every word I sang. Perhaps they did, in a way. The messages in the songs were about love and peace.

Words cannot describe sufficiently the grandeur I experienced of the Swiss Alps on my way from Italy to Switzerland. I live in the Rocky Mountains, so I had grown up with a respect and awe for God's majestic fortresses. No wonder ancient prophets retreated to those high places for solitude and inspiration. Small villages adorned my paths in the Swiss mountains. They were paved with cobblestone streets. The stones were shiny from decades of wear. Families provided room and board. I shared my music again with them and exchanged dialogue about home, family, and occasionally the gospel. I left Switzerland for France, where my biggest performance would take place.

I sang at a government building on the Champs-Elysees, a large, robust and famous avenue in Paris, France. Experiences of the Eiffel Tower, museums, artwork, fashions, and the ballet developed into priceless memories. I shared my music many times and connected with people I had never seen before, who became something more than strangers through music. I looked at them as children of God, my brothers and sisters who were on the same journey of life that I was and who shared the same purpose for being on this earth.

The last place I visited was England. I found the language to be easier for communication, but the feeling of connection remained the same. I learned to express my feelings of gratitude to God for His creative masterpieces through my music. Everything happens for a reason.

In Ecclesiastes 3:1 I found this bit of wisdom: "To everything there is a season, and a time to every purpose under heaven." When I was first married and shortly after I had my oldest son, I became over-whelmed by perceived expectations that I had placed on myself. I was new to living a covenant life in the church. Being a perfection-ist didn't help with the demands that I placed on myself. I had a newborn and began reading every parenting book that I could get my hands on, including articles written about how to increase your child's IQ. My home was located in a moderate area of the city, and my ward was competitive, and not in a moderate way. It seemed that all the sisters I knew held two callings, attended the Temple twice a week, did compassionate service daily, kept an immaculate house, raised multitalented children, canned their own food that was grown in their own gardens, did their genealogy, and sewed all their own clothes, including the bedsheets.

I was hit with a tsunami of expectations that I thought I was obli-gated to meet. My wise mother sat me down and told me that there is a time and season for everything. She encouraged me to do the best I could and gave me her wisdom of how to be the best mom. I just needed to love my son. I didn't need all the books and articles that I was reading. She also gave me the advice to stop comparing myself to others. I needed to understand that I was unique and my offering to the Lord would be enough. Everything would fall into place according to its season.

If we can effectively grasp and accept the wisdom of the scripture in Ecclesiastes and let it serve as a guide and roadmap for our journey, then we can understand storms and trials better, appreciate talents and blessings more deeply, and gain discernment and wisdom. It can navigate our course closer to becoming charitable and more like our Savior. Understanding that everything happens for a reason broadens our vision of the lessons we are to learn from our trials. It motivates us to heal by serving others. In Matthew 25:40, 45 we are told, "And the king shall answer and say unto them, verily I say unto you, Inasmuch as ye have done it unto one of the least of these my brethren, ye have done it unto me."

Every storm, every trial, test, and tragedy that my family or I faced in life was met with strength from gospel principles. Knowing that God's gift of the Atonement serves as a catalyst for healing, growth, and progress helped navigate our ship and played a huge part in our learning how to dance in the rain. When I accepted God's wisdom of having a time, season, and place for everything, I was able to sort things out. I was able to approach problems with less anxiety and have more hope and faith in my abilities. I could say to myself, "Okay, I can do this!" Learning to have a desire to do service and give up the selfish tendencies of our human nature is a continual challenge. Sometimes it comes naturally, and at other times it is more coerced. Yes, everything happens for a reason.

I continued magnifying and sharing my music throughout college. I had the privilege of singing with the Mormon Youth Choir. It was one of the most intimidating and frightening auditions I had ever experienced. The results were positive, and it became one of the most rewarding times in my life. I was trying to gain the courage to try out for the Tabernacle Choir later in my life. Again, extensive preparation began with music training, performing, and studying. It became intense, because I was also pursuing a degree in nursing, something I really wanted, and the timeframe seemed right for me.

I sang in General Conference several times, at Disneyland, with the Tab Choir, and made several recordings. One of the most memorable was a performance of Handel's *Messiah* at Christmastime with the Tabernacle Choir. All this kindled the craving and desire I had for music and performing. I had plans and a determination to complete them. I would soon learn the significance of the wisdom, "there is a time and season for everything."

My plans took a detour after I decided to marry and begin my family. My focus became solely on family, not myself. I began moving toward another season in my life with wonderful dreams ahead, coupled by high expectations. As I was building my family, I kept music alive and part of my being. I wrote a few songs, instructed students on the guitar, and participated in performing whenever I was asked. It was the season to share my music in a way that would last for generations. Serving my family by teaching the love of music to them, in my way, was using the calm and peace that comes from accepting the Lord's time frame. It helped my children learn and gain an appreciation for music and talent. I was able to pass on respect for gifts of talent and a desire to use that talent to help and enrich other lives. I wasn't able to complete my dream of being in the Tabernacle Choir, but I made dreams of a more significant kind in that season of time. Service comes in all sorts of colors and shapes. Everything happens for a reason.

During the season of raising my family, I was able to use the athletic talents that had been shelved since high school. I worked several hours a week to provide the monetary means for all of my children to participate in extracurricular activities. My daughters became well rounded with opportunities in dance, music, and athletics. My sons explored sports, music, and Scouts. There were many hours spent bonding with them as I supported, practiced with, and sometimes coached them. I was an avid skier, and when in college, I went to the slopes every weekend. I had the money to enjoy that sport. But when I had a family, the budget did not allow that luxury. Sacrifices were made willingly so I was able to teach my children how to ski and snowboard. There is a season for everything. Watching them grow, learn, and experience the satisfaction of success and accomplishment was a blessing and reward I cherish. I feel that I served my family by using talents that I had been given early on in life, talents that had been groomed for a higher purpose than I understood at that time. Everything happens for a reason.

Just as we all have been given talents, we all have purpose. I feel we are gently guided, through the gospel of Jesus Christ, to fulfill our purpose here on earth. I feel that by trying our best to be like the Savior, we are able to survive the Refiner's fire and make the world a better place. We have purpose. We have meaning. They each become accentuated in the season they are needed.

In Alma 26:6 we are given a preview of our times and the conditions that we will face and the trials we will be weathering. It states: "Yea they shall not be beaten down by the storm at the last day; yea, neither shall they be harrowed up by the whirlwinds; but when the storm cometh they shall be gathered together in their place, that the storm cannot penetrate, to them; yea, neither shall they be driven with fierce winds whithersoever the enemy listed to carry them." This is a beautiful promise of hope. We are promised that we can survive the devastating effects of monstrous storms by gathering together in our place. What is that place? I truly believe that this is symbolic. Our place is our purpose. Our reason for being becomes our strength and fortitude when we comprehend who we are and we grasp through knowledge and experience our Heavenly Father's plan. Everything is carefully and spiritually calculated. God is a God of order. Everything happens for a reason.

We are all subjected to bad weather and storms. And we are also given agency to choose how to respond to these events. We can either completely surrender ourselves to the variable, unpredictable, and uncontrollable effects of weather and storms or we can choose to become independent from the ill effects they may have on our lives. We can prepare by dressing appropriately, securing our property and belongings, and providing for the temporal needs of our loved ones and ourselves. We can physically prepare, but how do we prepare mentally and spiritually?

We prepare mentally and spiritually by coming unto Christ and knowing we are children of God. We have purpose and intention. Nothing in this universe is here by chance. Our Earth was created by God to serve a purpose. We were endowed by our Creator with human traits of love, compassion, perseverance, and the ability to become like our Creator. It was never intended that we come to earth and float in an effortless environment of physical, emotional, and spiritual pleasures. We are here to be tried and tested. We are here to gain a body. We are here to have purpose, and we are here to make a difference. We need to pull ourselves together and realize that there is purpose to the challenges in life. The disappointments, sorrows, and pain we experience are flames of the Refiner's fire. They are meant to temper us, not consume us. A verse from Thomas Kelly's "Zion Stands with Hills Surrounded" speaks of the Refiner's furnace: "In the furnace God may prove thee, Thence to bring thee forth more bright, But can never cease to love thee; Thou art precious in His sight. God is with thee, God is with thee; Thou shalt triumph in his might." We must find a way to turn storms into blessings; blessings of strength and growth that will allow us to say, "Let it rain!" "I've got this." Everything happens for a reason, especially us.

Faith, Not Fear

IN THE NEW Testament, 2 Timothy 1:7, states: "For God hath not given us the spirit of fear; but of power, and of love, and of a sound mind." He has given us the ability, through agency, to choose whether to have faith or to be fearful. There is a hymn that speaks about faith and fear. It is simple and short but carries a deep, penetrating message. The first line of "When Faith Endures," begins by saying, "I will not doubt, I will not fear; God's love and strength are always near." This is the gift the apostle Paul was speaking of in the letter to his son, Timothy. The powerful gifts God has given us that enable us to conquer fear are His undying love and the guidance of the Holy Spirit. This love and guidance is our strength. It helps to lay our foundation for our relationship with God and helps us to come unto Christ. Peace of mind encircles our whole being when we put our trust in God and humbly pray for His direction. In navigating our ship through life's storms, we need a strong will and enduring faith. God's "love assures that fear departs when faith endures."

Fear is a tool of Satan. Just by its literal spelling the dangers of fear are evident. When we are prodded and enticed by fear, fault-finding becomes evident in our behavior. We find fault with ourselves, with others, with neighbors, friends and leaders. *Fault-finding* becomes a negative habit; degrading our very being. This is what the letter F stands for in the word *fear*. The letter E stands for another tool of the Adversary, *expecting* failure. We all have a tendency to not even try because we expect to fail, therefore discouragement sets in our souls. Our progress becomes stifled. Another common tool that Satan uses against us is distraction. We lose our focus on the big picture and who we are when we *allow distractions* to consume us, hence, A in the word *fear*. And finally, the last letter, R, in the word *fear* symbolizes our *resistance of the Spirit*. Sometimes we tell ourselves we are not worthy of the Spirit's guidance or that God doesn't love us, all tools of the Adversary. *Fear* is not only a negative word but it is also a negative and paralyzing action. It can have devastating effects, much like a ship running into an iceberg. That iceberg can either stop your ship in its tracks or, worst case scenario, it could sink your ship into depths of despair.

We have been given many tools and gifts from our Father in Heaven to combat fear. The first commandment tells us to love God with all our being and to put Him first. The first letter in the word *faith* is F. *First comes God.* We are told that if we first seek the things of the kingdom of God, other needs and concerns will fall into place and be taken care of by the Lord, especially through His Atonement. A is the second letter in the word *faith*. We need to *allow the atonement* to be a part of our life, our character, and our purpose. Coming unto Christ and accepting His Atonement paves the way for us to have increased faith, love, and peace of mind throughout our entire journey on this earth. The Atonement can heal and cleanse, give rest, restore, teach, and provide tender mercies; and direct and deepen testimony. This miraculous gift from our Lord and Savior is the foundation of our faith. It leads into the next letter I. Part of having faith is having the desire and the ability to *involve* yourself in positivity. I believe that people who have a positive attitude have faith. Positivity is an attitude that affects our environment, esteem, goals, dreams, values, visions, and behaviors. Positivity is a large part of faith. We must choose to embrace it, surround ourselves with it, and make it a habit daily. The next letter in the word *faith* is T, which encompasses *trust*. Trust is the ability to rely on someone and have confidence in their integrity. Trust must be earned and given with caution. It can be hard to trust if you have had that trust broken, especially by someone you love. But when we are asked to trust in the Lord, we do so knowing that He loves us unconditionally and that He will always be there for us. He *is* truth and integrity. He is the one being that we can trust wholeheartedly and know that trust will never be broken. And the last letter of *faith* is H, which represents *hope*. By having faith we are able to hope for a brighter future, to see a calming of the storm, to feel relief from pain and suffering, and to see our own potential, worth, and purpose. The answer is "Faith, not fear."

President Gordon B. Hinckley taught us a valuable truth when he said, "I am asking that we stop seeking out the storms and enjoy more fully the sunlight. I am suggesting that as we go through life we 'accentuate the positive' . . . . that optimism replace pessimism, that faith exceed our fears." This beautiful concept of having and developing faith can be our guiding star, serve as our anchor, become our source of energy and strength, and be our most valued among our "tools of the trade." Faith serves two purposes by definition. Faith is a noun and can represent confidence and trust, or it can be a belief that is not based on proof or a belief in doctrines or a code of ethics. It can stand for a belief in God and an obligation and loyalty to Him. Faith is also a verb and action word when it is considered to be a sacred act. It is concrete motivation for positive behaviors. It is the driving force that provides a forward movement in our journey. It is a fuel for our eternal progression and the wind blowing consistently against our sails to move and guide our ship. Faith is what allows us to set goals, make plans, dream, and embrace positivity. "Faith, not fear."

Setting goals is an act of faith. All through the scriptures we find instructions, commandments, and plans that are goals in one form or another. By setting goals we are exercising our faith and learning to self-reflect so we can prioritize events and actions in our lives. We can learn to accomplish and experience the joy of keeping the commandments and putting God first by having faith to set goals. There is an old adage that states "First things first." An adage is usually a philosophical saying that communicates an important truth. In the scriptures we are taught that Jesus Christ is truth and light. He is Alpha and Omega. He is the First and the Last. The commandments put worshiping God as the first and greatest commandment. In setting priorities, it is essential to put God and Jesus Christ first in our lives. Christ has said, "Find me first, and then you will find yourself."

Through prayer and listening to the Spirit, we can all see clearly about what our priorities should be and how to act on them, which becomes the first step in setting goals. Having a pronounced self-awareness is the next step. Know yourself. Inquire of God to have a conviction of your worth and value. Journal your thoughts and inspirations and then use them to guide you in setting priorities and goals. Explore your visions, values, dreams, and mission. After you become well-acquainted with each, take action on every one of them. Setting goals is an act of faith and also a continuous process that we all go through during our lifetime. Each phase of our lives is tailored by precise goals and priorities, ones that are in season and timed appropriately. Sometimes plans become diverted and we need to tweak our goals and update a few of our priorities. It is always good to have a plan A, B, and even a C.

When I was raising my family after my divorce, I became overwhelmed with tasks, responsibilities, and expectations. I was working three nursing jobs, trying to hold down a church calling, raising five children, cooking, cleaning, shopping, and doing yard work; you name it. I needed to be organized and frugal. I needed stability and balance in my life. I went to the Lord often and cried to Him about my concerns of inadequacy. I desperately needed guidance and tools that I could use to accomplish what I needed for my family and myself. Through prayer and reading the scriptures I was directed to reach deep inside and explore some self-awareness. I discovered that with the Lord's help, I had strengths that I didn't realize. Daily inspiration came, and I listened intensely to the Spirit for direction. It didn't come right away. Sometimes it required a ritual of repetition, trying and failing, and then trying again before I understood what I was supposed to do. Finally I was inspired to identify my priorities and just begin.

Putting God first was always priority number one. The next became effective time management. We are all given the same twenty-four hours in our day, and those precious hours are spent in a unique way. I had very limited time in one day to do a decent job with all my responsibilities. Often I would read my Patriarchal Blessing for encouragement. It cautioned me to be prayerful, always.

Gradually, through reading, prayer, and picking other people's brains for ideas, I slowly came up with ideas for time management. I had a large home, and cleaning it took several days. Laundry was always included in this huge project. You can imagine how much laundry I had with five children. Three daily loads was not an exaggeration. To accomplish my enormous task, I set goals for each room in my home and the laundry. I prioritized what was to be done in each room. Directions were simple and written on a small bright-colored piece of cardstock. It was then attached to the back of a cupboard door in each room. All were color-coordinated to the day of the week with each day represented by a different color. They were also categorized by daily chores, weekly tasks, and monthly projects. I eventually included meal preparation using this particular method. It worked well and it relieved the pressure I had put on myself. My tasks became bearable, and using this method made it easier to feel I was actually accomplishing something. My children were included in doing chores and meal planning. I probably exaggerated this concept a bit, because my children have all told me that I was obsessed with organization. It's true. I color-coordinated closets and picture-labeled containers so clean up could be faster and easier.

A well-planned schedule of events and important appointments hung on my pantry door. All the children had their own color. Laundry baskets, chores, and events were tied to that particular color. Rewards were given when chores were done, and privileges were denied when things were neglected. This method was not perfect, but it worked for me. It was an answer to a prayer and a result of hard work, compromise, and faith. "Faith, not fear."

My next priority in my goal-setting endeavor became spiritual health for my family and myself. I perceived and thought I was expected to play the role of mother and father. The thought brought me to my knees in tears. I had lost a part of me, and my children had holes in their hearts that would be hard to fill. When growing up, I had been taught to make God, spirituality, and my faith priorities. It had never been difficult until now. For some reason it seemed hard and nearly impossible. That is until the Spirit helped me to realize that this feeling or fear was coming from the Adversary. Again I looked deep inside myself to determine what spiritual health meant to me and what I wanted to accomplish. I felt that my number-one priority was to keep my Temple covenants. I knew that doing so would give me the strength, blessings, and guidance that I needed for my family and myself. I set time aside to go to the Temple. It had to be on a night that I could have my parents, sister, or a babysitter watch my children. The Lord helped me accomplish that goal. And that goal led to being creative about having Family Home Evening. To gather my "flock" once a week was quite a task. It took a lot of planning, prayer, and yes, some bribing to make it happen. But when it did, it was totally worth it and helped heal my family and me spiritually.

Setting goals for me always involved deep discussions with the Lord, because I truly felt I could not do it alone. I was able to get my children to have scripture study once a week as a family, but only if I bribed them with chocolate chip cookies. You have to do what you must, right? When it came to church attendance, it became a challenge extreme. I usually was exhausted Saturday evening, and by the time everyone took baths or showers and readied themselves for bed, I was near collapse. I carry guilt to this day because back then I didn't consider Sunday the day of rest it should have been. We made it through these rough waters of our journey, though. Before I finalized my divorce, I had a serious conversation with the Lord where I promised to teach my children the gospel of Jesus Christ with all my heart, I only needed His help, so He gave it to me.

When it came time for my sons to go on missions, I often worried that I hadn't taught them enough of the gospel or bore my Testimony often enough for them to make righteous decisions. But I realized that I did my best and they had their free agency. They chose to serve the

Lord by going on a mission for the right reasons, because they wanted to and they had the values of the gospel of Jesus Christ seeped into their core.

Those two goals, time management and spiritual health, became increasingly important, not only while I was raising my children, but also later, when they served as a compass of righteousness for my family. They gently guided us through a rough storm and helped us stay focused on our destiny. "Faith, not fear."

Change is hard, especially when it comes at an inconvenient time or it blindsides you unexpectedly. Setting goals helps you not only accomplish more but to also set standards for good habits and routines. It helps navigate you through the changing storms that are certain to come.

Raising my family in our home of thirty years was challenging. Changes came often of which we had to adapt. That was part of our journey, part of life. When I remarried, it was a huge change for my children, and goalsetting became a couple's endeavor, a partnership. Luckily my husband and I shared the same spiritual goals, which made life much easier. We made our children our priority, because of the great love we had for them. We set goals and priorities with the gospel principles at the helm. Together we tried hard to raise our family with unconditional love in an atmosphere of righteousness, which did not stop the storms from coming into our lives. Storms caused us to step back and reevaluate our priorities and tweak our plans and even reset our goals. Conflict came from differences in parenting methods, interests, and finances. Our faith was challenged. Constantly we were faced with the evil effects of divorce.

Both of us worked—full-time and part-time respectively—which tipped the clock away from favoring time spent with our children. Visitations became a timely, major repair job. After my children would come back from their visitation with their dad, I had to deal with acting out, disrespect, contention, and disobedience. It was like I had built a tall Lego tower and my ex-husband knocked it down, thus making me start all over again. After I remarried, my goals and priorities for spiritual health had not changed. These goals still gave us strength. We just had to try harder, pray more often, and be consistent. Our family grew; some got married, while others left home to pursue their own journeys in life. Those changes came; they couldn't be stopped. We held onto our hope and faith that our children would be successful and the Lord would watch over them and bless them. Change did not and should not affect your ability to give unconditional love. "Faith, not fear."

When we lost our home, we were forced into a frantic mode. We had to find a place to live immediately, get new jobs, and plan a way to survive financially. I still can envision the yellow eviction notice plastered to my front door. The memory of this event causes nauseated anxiety to settle in at my very core. After the initial shock, I sat down and had another deep and serious conversation with the Lord. My soul was wounded deeply, and I mourned the loss of my home. It sickened me to watch so many of my cherished belongings be given away or sold. The Lord knew my pain and suffering. Every night I prayed that He would help me change my attitude so I wouldn't become bitter and I would be able to keep my faith and stay positive. After my conversation with the Lord, I sat down and made a priority list, a "to do" list, if you will.

Finding a place to live was top priority. A rental home became available that suited our needs. Family, friends, and ward members helped us move. My children's friends came from unexpected places to give their assistance. The house was not big enough to store all of our belongings, so we had to rent several storage sheds. I eventually found myself standing inside the new house. Breathing became hard and my eyes opened wide as I surveyed the cumbersome tasks that lay before me. Towers of boxes formed obstacles everywhere. I began to cry. Then I remembered having that same overwhelming feeling just after my divorce. I recalled how much the Lord had helped me, and peace came over me. It seemed He was reminding me that I needed to have faith and "just do it."

Our surroundings eventually took shape and started to resemble a personalized home. We worked relentlessly to make it our own and took pride in our accomplishments. Holidays were warm and inviting; the neighbors welcoming and kind. I gave to the neighbors many Christmas lights that I could no longer use. Our whole street looked like a light show at Christmas, and it brought a lot of joy into peoples' lives. Laughter emerged, and I finally started to feel positive energy return.

I had acquired an adjunct professorship at a local university. Teaching at the university became the love of my life. I really felt I was making a difference in my students' lives. I was able to show them how much I loved nursing and help them decide what kind of nurse they wanted to be. I expected high standards from my students, because they were embarking on a profession that required compassion, precision, and good judgment. They taunted me often by claiming I was a difficult instructor. Later, at the end of the semester, those same students thanked me for what I had taught them. They said they would be better nurses because of me. That news was incredibly rewarding.

While we were in this rental home, my husband worked in North Dakota in the oil fields. It was an exhausting challenge. When we lost our home, savings, and retirement, it just about destroyed us financially. The venture in North Dakota was the only way we could see ourselves out of the dilemma, so we persevered for the next four years. He traveled back and forth from Utah to North Dakota. It was a strenuous storm to bear and a lonely one, but I kept my focus and drew strength from my faith. The storm grew and raged forward. I was laid off from the university because of financial issues and because I was the lowest professor on the "totem pole." I was not asked to come back to teach. It broke my heart. We were back in a dire financial situation again. At the same time I injured my knee and required surgery. As I was recuperating from the surgery, we received notice that we had to move. The home we had been renting was being foreclosed on because the owner had not been paying the mortgage payments with our rental payments. He had been paying on a home in Las Vegas that he owned. Oh, wow! Another storm. Now what?

I sat in my living room reclined in my rocker with my knee elevated and an ice machine attached to my knee. I asked the Lord, "How am I supposed to do this?" The answer came: "Faith, not fear."

I began making arrangements for my belongings to be packed and gradually was able to walk a little bit. Again, goals and priorities became a must. We were shackled to a time limit and my husband could not be there to help me move. It was going to be up to my family, friends, and me. Priority number one again became to find a place to live. Our stake had just been divided, and I received a call from my new bishop one evening. He told me that he had located another house for us to rent. It was located in the same stake. Another tender mercy from the Lord and answered prayers.

In the next few weeks our belongings were packed up and moved to a new location. We had to adapt quickly to this situation. We were making good money at that time, which allowed us to hire a moving company for the major moving that took place over the next few weeks. My organizational skills that I developed just after my divorce, now proved to be valuable. The process began all over again: move, clean, organize, and personalize. Even though these storms were vicious and inconvenient, I did recognize the hand of the Lord and His tender mercies throughout these experiences. Maybe it's a good thing that these events happened so quickly after the loss of our home. I was kept so busy that I did not have time to let bitterness or anger cloud my perspectives. I didn't have time to mourn a huge loss. "Faith, not fear."

After things began to settle somewhat, I began taking my resume around to different facilities for the purpose of acquiring employment. Beginning early in the morning and continuing into the afternoon became a daily ritual for weeks. I kept getting the response of "You are overqualified" or "We can't afford you." Discouragement soon set in, and I became depressed. We were starting to climb out of the financial doom we were in, but I still needed to bring in some income to help. I was getting older and tired and couldn't understand why my experience as a nurse didn't lead me to a good job. I decided to take it to the Lord.

I went to the Temple on a Thursday evening, and when I was in the Celestial Room I conversed through prayer. I told my Heavenly Father that I was physically tired and worn out and that my health was suffering. I explained my need for stability with our finances, yet less stress than I had at my nursing job. I told the Lord that I would go where He wanted me to go and where I was needed. I literally surprised myself that these thoughts and commitments came from my mouth, because I was extremely discouraged.

That Sunday, my bishop approached me about a job for which he wanted me to apply. He told me that it consisted of working for the Church in a managing position. I questioned his reasoning because I had no experience with retail, only nursing. But I remembered the Temple experience that I had a few days prior. I agreed to apply.

Soon I was called for an interview. After the interview I was asked by a brother from Salt Lake City why I applied for the job. He stated that the church could not pay me what my nursing job had paid me and wondered why a seasoned experienced nurse would seek out that type of employment. I told him about my Temple experience and explained that I had a varied amount of managing skills, and if they could be of help, I would be happy to assist. I also said that I understood if they could not acquire me as an employee. I then went home thinking I would not get a call back. The next morning I received a call and they offered me the job with an increase in salary because of my skills. "Faith, not fear."

The Lord had directed me to a place where He wanted me to be and I spent the next seven years in an environment that was totally different from any work environment I had ever been in. Our staff had morning and afternoon devotionals. The feeling and atmosphere of the Center was sacred and spiritual. My family noticed a huge difference in my countenance and demeanor. Stress levels plummeted, and I was happy and felt safe. I met extraordinary people who were willing to give outstanding service to the Lord. I grew both spiritually and intellectually. Strong relationships were formed as I was privileged to work closely with the temple presidency, stake presidents and other church leaders. My testimony soared. I became humble and more teachable than I had ever been. Constantly I marveled at the inspiration, dedication, and organization of the administration of the church. My skills increased tenfold. Finally I was not considered to be computer illiterate by my children.

Watching and experiencing the lives of the people I worked with caused me to gain confidence in humanity. I loved every minute of every day that I spent there. Even though my life had taken a positive turn and my environment was serene, I was still hit with several storms while there. Again I was faced with adversity and had the choice to embrace the valuable lessons that these storms would teach.

Life has been a constant struggle for some of my children. My youngest son is autistic and has struggled forging through life since he was young. Suffering from the separation of hospital stays, the confusion he feels about expectations and his abilities has taken a toll on his self-esteem. When he was a teenager, he became more and more irritable in crowds, and his fear of failure increased. Helping him get through a school day was extremely traumatic.

We watched as he gradually sank into despair. For his mental health we removed him from high school in the eleventh grade. The next three years were spent helping him earn a driving license. Simple things we all take for granted were difficult for him. His social skills were thin and in some instances non-existent. He stopped going to church because he felt very uncomfortable and would experience meltdowns. He was doing well in Scouts until a leader told him he wasn't Scout material, which just solidified his feelings of inadequacy. My feelings of anger and disappointment set in toward this leader. I tried desperately to understand him and forgive him for injuring my child. This leader had shown up at my work to inform me that he didn't feel my son should return to Scouts, which ended the last influence the gospel would have on his life, in a collective sense. My thoughts were plagued with questions of "Why?" and "How could you?" I didn't receive any answers or peace at that time, so I just refocused my time and energy toward my son and his needs. When

I was working at the Center, my son went through several jobs as he tried to be independent. He could focus on only one main event at a time. He either concentrated on his job or getting his GED. It seemed he always chose his job, because he was terrified of failure. He made slow, cumbersome progress and eventually saw some tiny successes.

A mother's heart is broken when she has to watch her child suffer and struggle with self-worth. My heart broke and I was sad when he suffered, but it swelled with pride when he made progress. He still willingly participated in family prayer and blessings on the food. His prayers were stiff and versed but were said with a humble heart and willing spirit. I was proud of him. A fond memory I had while at the Center was when he brought me lunch as a surprise. One time he actually gave me a big hug, which was miraculous, because he had not wanted to be touched, ever. When he willingly put his arms around me, I was brought to tears. I have dreams and aspirations for my son. He is still continuing his journey. When I am strong in my faith and exhibit well-being, he is able to stay focused and have a desire to move forward. When I am sad or stressed, it seems to have a negative effect on him, so my presence at the Center had a good effect on everyone, because I was positive. "Faith, not fear."

Some memorable and uplifting events took place while I served at the Center. I say served because it felt more like a calling than a job. Several of my grandchildren were baptized into the Church of Jesus Christ of Latter-Day Saints. I had the privilege of engraving their names on a set of scriptures for each of them. It was something I could do, and I felt I was giving a part of me that they could remember for a long time. It was special to see the gold lettering expressing their names on the Word of God and knowing that they had made the decision to take upon them the name of Christ. More tender mercies from the Lord.

Another incredible event took place. My youngest daughter and future son-in-law were shopping for items for their wedding reception. I willingly tagged along. Hours were spent looking for the perfect dress, shoes, and accessories. Both of them made their way to the checkout counter with their arms draped with clothing and items to be purchased. I stood back away from the crowd.

Instantly I felt as if someone was watching me and turned quickly to look over my shoulder. My heart sank, and I reversed my view, to hide my face from the individual who was staring at me. She slowly approached me and leaned over, calling me by name. Timidly she asked if we could talk. I didn't respond because I didn't know what to say. It was the woman who, along with my ex-husband, destroyed my marriage and disrupted my children's lives. The woman had given me only frail and meaningless excuses for her affair with my husband.

I clenched my lips. "I guess. I don't really think there is much to talk about."

"I don't blame you for feeling that way." I could barely hear her response. She began by asking for my forgiveness for the pain and suffering she caused me and my family. She apologetically explained that she had been brought up better and knew what she did was wrong. As she spoke I felt an invisible bubble form around us. Sound was muffled, and all I could hear was our conversation. The Spirit enveloped both of us and touched our hearts. I fought back tears as I felt the anxiety and uneasiness leave my body. The words "I forgive you" surprisingly were uttered from me, and we embraced. Kind expressions of concern were exchanged, and she departed. I finally felt because of this experience that I could forgive my ex-husband and move forward. "Faith, not fear."

My youngest daughter was married. She was blessed to be married in our local Temple, and she was radiant. A beautiful reception was held in my sister's backyard. Crowds of friends and family members were there to support her, including most of the workers from the Center. She and her new husband lived with us for a while. I was grateful we could help out. I felt blessed. Life was calm and serene. History does repeat itself, and we were certainly not left out of that scenario.

The next few storms on my horizon were huge and cantankerous. They all happened within a few years of each other, and frankly

I could barely function. While busy trying to maneuver my life situations and traumas, I never lost sight of my children's dreams and aspirations. Gradually I was blessed with grandchildren whom I was able to give the same considerations. I think we all dream and plan our lives, set goals, and act on ideas that we work toward making a reality. We do the same with our children. When those dreams stagger and fade, we feel a myriad of things—sadness, confusion, heartache, and yes, sometimes a tinge of disappointment. Those things are natural but at some point we need to gather up the unconditional love we have for those suffering and let our faith buoy us up. There are moments when we feel we don't have the strength, but we find that we really do, if we rely on the Lord.

I remember the storm that hit when we had to remove my son from high school, and I mourned the loss of the dreams I had for him. It stung! It hurt! It made me question my qualities as a mother. We try hard to do what is best for our children and pour out all the love we have for them, and it becomes almost devastating and paralyzing when we can't change circumstances or situations that are causing them pain.

There was a nightmare of a storm that hit our family. We were coming back from the airport. It was dark and rain was drizzling down. My middle daughter was ending a shift at work, and we were headed home. The atmosphere in the car was heavy and there was an uncomfortable amount of silence. My daughter finally got the courage to tell me the reason for her somberness. She had become pregnant. Because she was a single women, this news definitely became a game changer for all of us, but especially for her. I remember taking some slow, deep breaths and thinking intensely about my response. Then was not the time to lecture or reprimand her, for I knew in my heart that it was very painful for my daughter to go through. She had been raised with unconditional love and deserved it then more than ever. I asked about the circumstances and the father. I was horrified at her response. The father was against keeping the baby and wanted her to have an abortion. He threatened abandonment if she did not comply. She volunteered her decision to me. She told him no, that she did not believe in abortion, and she was going to keep the baby. I was prepared for her decision if it were to go either way; I respected her agency. But I cried when she told me that she had decided against it. They were tears of joy.

A few seconds elapsed before I said anything to her. I looked her in the eyes and said that I was proud of her for making the decision that she did. I told her that I knew it was an extremely difficult one and that the road ahead would be challenging and hard. I then offered my love and support and told her that her family would help and do what they could. We did. My daughter stayed with her older sister until the baby was born. Her sister and I were there at my grandson's birth. My daughter has been brave.

She is the most kind and loving mother, and my grandson is such a blessing in our lives. It has been difficult and challenging for her, but she is amazing. Nelson Mandela said, "I learned that courage was not the absence of fear, but the triumph over it. The brave man is not he who does not feel afraid, but he who conquers that fear." My daughter embraced the challenge of conquering her fear and has done it with grace and dignity. "Faith, not fear."

You know, each one of us have gigantic, monstrous storms hit either us or our family members. Life is about choices, faith, and learning from those choices. Take time to dance in the rain and appreciate the now. Recognize the tender mercies and blessings we receive each day. It helps in the navigation of your ship through unpredictably rough waters.

I often wondered while I was at the Center how I could feel such peace and yet be tossed among billows and raging torrents of rain. I know my Savior was helping steer my ship. I was navigated by faith, and perseverance became the wind on my sail. But I had bouts of exhaustion where I just wanted a break. But that break did not come.

I have always had a close relationship with all of my children. Each relationship is unique and centered on their personality, their place in the family sequence, and their needs. I developed a uniquely close relationship with my oldest daughter. We became good friends as she matured and grew into adulthood. Her childhood was seeped with memories of dance, sports, talent in music, student government, and just being a kind and intelligent human being. She had always come to my defense and was extra sensitive to her surroundings. It was her wedding reception that was held in the backyard of the home I lost. She was the first of my children to be married. She is the mother of my first grandchild.

Using her talents, my daughter, along with her husband, has created and produced a beautiful family. They have had their challenges, like most. I watched my daughter grow in knowledge and testimony throughout her teenage years and young adulthood. She was inquisitive and not afraid to explore new ideas and concepts. Her countenance shone with love and life. I never felt that I had to worry about her convictions to the gospel of Jesus Christ. I felt she and her husband were strong individuals with good judgment. The thought of them taking a different course in life never occurred to me; in fact it not once gave me cause for concern. The distance we experienced, physically, made relationships hard, but not impossible. Contact and conversations were made as often as possible. Their family expanded to three girls and a rambunctious set of identical twin boys. Life became extremely busy and demanding for my daughter. It possibly became overwhelming.

When I look back on this storm I regret that I became so involved in my world at my feet that I was complacent about her situation. I missed something. I will forever ask myself what and wrestle with questions that weigh heavy on my heart. My daughter and her dear husband made a choice to separate themselves and their children from the Church of Jesus Christ of Latter-Day Saints. I'm sure it was not a decision that was made lightly or without thought, but I can say that when the news came to me, I was certainly without words. I had to respect their agency and their choice. I was told that it was about them and not me. It hurt with a sting that burnt deeply. You see, I had been raised and I raised my family to realize that every decision you make in life affects those around you, especially those who love you. Our family dynamics were tousled and upset. I was confused. I felt that I could no longer discuss and share concepts of the gospel or relate my testimony to my daughter and my grandchildren.

It was so difficult to find a balance, and it took time before our relationship was normalized again. I desperately hung on to the closeness and unconditional love I had for them. I respect the wonderful people that they are and find peace in knowing they are strong. They are in my thoughts and prayers on a daily basis, for I want their happiness and success. I've grown tired of the sleepless nights and the tears. I search for answers, answers that may never come. I focus on the positive and the now. I couldn't love a child more than I love my daughter and her family. I know that my feelings are natural and that someday I will come to the knowledge and understanding that I need. My love will never change for her and my concerns will never end. I pray they will find the answers that they need and that God will continue to direct their ship through their storms. This storm may not have been theirs, from their perspective, but it developed into mine.

When you feel helpless and like you just can't navigate life and fear envelopes your whole being that is when you need the Savior the most and He will carry you. His answers will always be the same to your questions, "Faith, not fear."

I have always worried and been concerned about all my children. The principles in the *Proclamation of the Family* teach us that family is an eternal concept and is sacred. Families grow generation by generation and literally extend into eternity. My family didn't end when I was married, and I don't believe my children's ended when they were married. Love is eternal and so is a mother's worry.

Thinking that my youngest daughter was on her way to a strong beginning with her own family made it so I didn't worry with exasperation. From all outward appearances, life was good. We also had a strong relationship. She and her husband lived close, so family get-togethers were frequent. I looked forward to playing games and our visits. Ambition was a part of both my daughter's and her husband's nature. She worked full-time and he worked and studied. His plans were to attend law school.

It seems this storm came out of nowhere. It reminded me of the storms that hit Lake Powell when we were there. The storms would come suddenly from seemingly nowhere and violently cause damage to everyone in its path. The dark clouds and wind were warnings to seek shelter immediately. Something happened that no mother wants to see a child go through, a divorce. I had "been there, done that," and I pleaded with the Lord to brace my daughter with His love and mend her broken heart.

Satan is the father of all lies. When someone succumbs to temptations and becomes fully engulfed in lies, they surrender to the Evil one. The light of Christ becomes dim and the Spirit withdraws. There were lies that seeped into her husband's being, lies about his worthiness, faithfulness, and daily activities. Just as pornography became a cancer for my ex-husband, so lying and deceit became her husband's cancer. It spread rapidly through their marriage and eventually was its demise. He had cruelly taken her wedding ring and left their apartment permanently. Cheating on his wife took place often, but the horror my daughter had to face was abuse. He almost put her in the hospital on more than one occasion. Taking on a false identity on the internet became a game to him and led to more infidelity. Because his father was a lawyer in town with some prestige, nothing surfaced about the abuse and was hidden, and divorce papers were drawn up and signed without my daughter having any representation. He served her the divorce papers on Christmas Eve.

Months were spent talking until late hours. Boxes of Kleenex were stockpiled. She and I went through mounds of comfort food. Blessings were given and prayers were said on her behalf. She exhibited a strong, persevering spirit.

I found myself telling my beautiful daughter the same things my mother lovingly told me when I went through my divorce. There is not a handbook on how to survive a divorce. If there was I think I would have acquired it a long time ago. Time heals. I bore my testimony to her about the Atonement and encouraged her to embrace it with all her heart. "Take time and reflect on the Atonement" was my weekly advice. I put my arms around her often to shelter her from pain and catch the falling tears. I would silently ask, "Oh, why did this happen?" It was a repetitive question that surfaced frequently. I knew in my heart that we don't always understand the whys. Instead I found myself telling her the things that I had echoing in my mind concerning positivity, knowing that I was a child of God and understanding the plan of salvation. Taking it an hour, a day at a time was a ritual. It was painful, but I watched my daughter grow and embrace her light and the Savior's promise through the Atonement. I learned from her how to forgive and move forward without guile. There is an unknown quote that I found, "Feed your faith and your fears will starve to death." She fed her faith daily, and eventually her fears subsided and faded. She is now blessed with a husband and three beautiful children. She is thriving and survived this crazy, wicked storm. "Faith, not fear."

Franklin D. Roosevelt was known for his famous saying, "The only thing we have to fear is fear itself." Fear is evil. It's a source of doubt. We can develop hate because we fear the unknown or what we do not understand. Nothing good comes from fear. We must shun it and master our fears. We are all familiar with this unfortunate feeling. You can find it can be the anchor to your biggest test. All these events that took place while I was at the Center were devastating and completely debilitating for moments at a time, but nothing quite compared to the ultimate test of my faith that came. Never before in my entire life had I feared losing my faith. I had weak moments but relied on my strong testimony to buoy me up until I could catch my breath on my own. I never felt that I would completely drown in my trials. Little did I know of the potential "iceberg" that lay ahead.

To promote good relations and concrete communications, I took on a project at the Center. My goal was to meet with every stake president in my temple district. There were seventeen, so it became an ominous task. I was excited and was really looking forward to it.

My communications had been through email or by phone up until now. It was also a project that I took on at the suggestion of my supervisor, who wanted me to develop some additional leadership skills. Our goal was to "Lead like the Savior," and it was a continual process. I began visits and they went well and were moderately successful. I was told from my first day on this job that leading like the Savior meant that you adopted His characteristics in your managing style. Every year I reviewed with my supervisor my accomplishments and areas where I needed to improve. Were there mistakes made? Of course. I worked vigorously. I had a couple of complaints that I knew about, which caused me concern and reflection. I felt I corrected the issues and continued. I never received negative reviews from my supervisors that weren't minor and that couldn't be easily corrected. I loved my staff and strived for honest feedback from them.

Unexpectedly my whole world came crashing down around me like never before. I had experienced criticism in my past and even had fought off disdain from a select few, but what I experienced next made me fear that I would lose my faith. Gossip causes carnage like no other. We are cautioned to avoid it at all costs. All of us are human, and some make better choices than others. Unfortunately gossip can intrude in our lives and rob us of justice. My situation became dire when I received a visit from my supervisor. I was given a verbal warning. I needed to correct my behavior. When I inquired as to what that might be, I was told that a stake president had heard that I was mean to my staff and fostered an atmosphere of hostility at the Center. I met these accusations with denial because they were untrue; however, I agreed to talk to the stake president and apologize and ask what he wanted me to improve.

I tried doing just that and was met with a cruel and demeaning response. I was told by this ecclesiastical leader that I was broken and irreparable. He then proceeded to tell me he didn't believe my apology was sincere and I needed to seek forgiveness. His goal was to remove me from my job because "the community deserves better." In the next few days he organized a meeting with all the stake presidents to hasten my removal. Many of them disagreed and felt the gesture was un-Christ like. One of them was my own stake president.

My stake president immediately contacted me after the meeting to give me a heads up and to tell me that he and many of the other stake presidents disagreed with this process. He even offered to contact my supervisor. I told him there was no need. I felt this had already gone too far; I didn't have a defense, and it was a case of "guilty until proven innocent." In my case no one questioned me or asked about my feelings, not one of my accusers. This stake president succeeded in removing me from the job that I loved. The hypocrisy that prevailed was insurmountable. I was expected to "Lead like the Savior," but was treated with un-Christ like harsh judgment. My supervisor hardly spoke to me when they came to dismiss me. I was embarrassed and humiliated beyond description. My staff was devastated. No one had answers or understood what was happening, especially not me.

I trudged to my car with my belongings and fighting back tears. I felt weak, angry, and defeated. One of my missionaries offered to take me home. I started crying so hard on the way that she had to pull over. It started to rain, and all I remember is the sound of the window wipers clunking against the windshield. My hand shaking, I made a call to my stake president. He was shocked and disappointed. Later, he gave me a blessing and cautioned me to not let anger cause me to be bitter or lose my faith. I'm afraid it was too late for that advice, even though I did appreciate it at the time.

Now what? This is not to bad-mouth my leaders or show disrespect to my church, but rather this writing is a proclamation of my success in overcoming adversity and coming back to my faith. I had to sort out the difference between the Church organization and the Gospel. The Church organization is phenomenal and unmatched in its accomplishments, charity, and general purpose. But with that being said, the people in the church are imperfect, and some are very wrong with the choices that they make. The Gospel of Jesus Christ is true. That is where the answers are, and it is through the Atonement that we heal and that we can become whole and one with Christ. The gospel principles give you peace when you feel despair and hope when you feel like you can't go on.

During the storms of my life, I felt many emotions: sorrow, fear, anger, betrayal, and doubt. I have learned valuable concepts of truth from all of my trials, including this one. Getting my self-worth back has been an upward climb. My ship was damaged temporarily, and it will take time and effort to repair it. Life is not the same for me. In some ways it is better. The Atonement has new and reinforced meaning for me. Agency dominates my will to see things go my way; a quickened understanding of unconditional love has emerged, and I have been blessed to know that the Lord compensates for our losses when we invite Him to do so. Returning to activity was my decision and was made only after considerable healing took place. I learned that my Savior understands me. He knows me and what I can endure. Through His grace and tender mercies I have been able to overcome my biggest fear—that of losing my faith. No storm can sink my ship. My ship moves forward with open sail, and the winds of adversity hasten my journey. Let the rain come! I will dance, and when I get tired, I will dance some more. "Faith, not fear."

Conclusion: Where There's a Will There's a Way

WHEN I WAS younger I was encouraged by my loving parents and motivated by them to reach my potential. They would often tell me, "You can become anything you want." I believed in that philosophy for a long time. After experiencing several disappointments in *not* becoming what I wanted to become, I realized there was much more involved than simply "wanting" it. We all want joy and happiness, success and achievement, peace and fulfillment. How we obtain these accomplishments, however, is as individualized as a thumbprint and DNA. Our journey begins when we are born. We enter this life with an innate will to live, to breathe in life experiences and find our way. Webster describes *will* as a desire or purpose having the "faculty of conscience" to deliberate and determine action. The word *way* is defined as a "journey, direction, course, or plan." It is very interesting to note that a *way* can also be "the timbers on which a ship is built and launched." When we left our Father in Heaven he gave us a plan or a way for us to find our course to return to Him. It involves building our lives or ship on a foundation of His plan, and Jesus Christ which will then launch us onto a strategic course to our heavenly home.

When a ship is launched, it is done so with advanced preparation. A barrage of inspections and tests are done on the vessel before it can embark on a journey. A strong individual is chosen as its captain, one with extensive knowledge of maps, sailing, and navigation. This same kind of planning went into the Plan of Happiness that was put forth in the preexistence. Our spirits were nurtured and inspected to determine our worthiness for the journey. We all decided and agreed to the conditions set forth for this miraculous adventure called life. The Captain for our journey was chosen, even Jesus Christ our Savior and the "captain of our souls." He alone has the knowledge, integrity, and navigational skills to guide our ship to its destination safely.

Launching our ship is the beginning of our life journey. We need the Savior at its helm and His guidance and skills to see us to our journey's end. Our crew consists of ourselves, our family, friends, and neighbors. The ship will not function well and with precision without a strong and determined crew. We must find our will early in our course and strengthen it continually. Finding that desire to serve God begins at an early age for all of us.

Babies are born in innocence, and every human being is endowed with a gift from God, the light of Christ. This divine gift serves as a conscience and litmus test for determining right from wrong and showing compassion for life. Depending on our circumstances and environment, this gift develops into a will fashioned by core values that are taught and wisdom that is acquired through life experiences. Some of us are very strong-willed and some flounder through life constantly trying to find their way. Connecting with God early in life serves to our advantage in developing a strong will. Finding your will becomes a choice. At some point in life we all must ask ourselves, "What do I want from life?" and "How do I want to be remembered?" You must make a conscious decision to serve God and accept Jesus Christ. This decision isn't always a "one-and-done" event. It comes in waves and phases and is tailored to what we are experiencing at the time. Our will becomes apparent when we embrace conversion. By giving ourselves to God and surrendering to His will, our desire is strengthened to serve Him and keep His commandments.

In the *Book of Mormon* Nephi and his family were asked to do and endure hard and dangerous things. 1 Nephi 3:7 states, "And it came to pass that I, Nephi, said unto my father: I will go and do the things which the Lord commanded for I know that the Lord giveth no commandments unto the children of men, save he shall prepare a way for them that they may accomplish the thing which he commandeth them." Nephi had already made his decision to serve the Lord and keep His commandments. His will evolved through faith. He made his decisions through prayer and then humbly set his number-one priority as putting God first. Nephi's desire, or will, through faith and prayer, helped him achieve his goal and put him on a righteous path, or way for his life journey. We can all be like Nephi. It begins by having or finding a desire to serve and know God. We need to live by the adage, "First things first." Our first should be God.

In order to set priorities, you need to explore who you are and who you want to become. Having knowledge of the concept that we are all sons and daughters of God is a perfect place to start. Self-awareness helps you be clearer about priorities and what direction you choose to sail on your journey through life. Knowing who you are will shape your visions, values, and dreams. It also develops a strong will and forms direction for your mission here on this earth. Trust in the Lord, as Nephi, and know you will not be going on this journey alone, for the Lord will provide a way for you to keep His commandments. We all have agency, another gift from God, that enables each of us to choose what actions to take toward each of the visions, values, and dreams that we might have. These are called goals. It is taught in the book *Preach My Gospel* that setting goals is an act of faith. When we set a goal, no matter how large or small, we must remember "where there's a will, there's a way."

God provides us with the knowledge of His will. He tells us in the scriptures that "It is my work and my glory to bring to pass the eternal life of man." He has made it clear what His will or desire and purpose is and He has also provided a way, the Plan of Salvation. As we journey through our lives we are constantly discovering our will and finding our way. As we do, we need to be aware of God's will and humble ourselves to it. The plan that He has set forth for us not only helps us develop a strong will but also procures a way and a course to follow.

The Doctrine and Covenants 63:20 states, "He that endureth in faith and doeth my will, the same shall overcome." No storm can tear you down, no devastation will be too deep, and no pain becomes unbearable when you humbly and sincerely desire to overcome. When you have a desire to accomplish something, you will find a way to remove doubt and obstacles. You will discover endless possibilities and experience joy when you find that with God nothing is impossible.

I imagine Nephi thought about this when he was commanded to build a ship to carry him and his family across an ocean with an unknown course. Or Moses as he brought the Israelites to the edge of the Red Sea and parted the waters for their safe crossing. In more modern times I think about Columbus venturing into an unknown world. With all of these instances, there was "a will and a way." God loves each of us individually, and our will, our plans, and our desires are of utmost importance to Him. He can help us overcome the obstacles that we face, conquer our fears, endure the storms that beat upon us, and master our faith. "Where there's a will, there's a way."

When the Lord commanded Nephi to build the ship that carried him across the ocean, he provided instruction for developing tools and fashioning the lumber used to construct a ship built like no other of its time. When we left the preexistence to embark on our life journey, we left with knowledge and instructions for building our ship. These instructions would come through scriptures, prophets, prayer, and inspiration. Like Nephi, some of the things we might hear or receive might be unpopular for our time or seem unusual and cause us to doubt or question. But because God loves us, He provides guidance and instructions for each step of our journey. With God, nothing is impossible. We all can successfully build our ships to be strong, durable and safe. These ships will carry our precious loved ones through vast waters of unknown and weather any storm that might envelope it. Our sails will be filled by the winds of adversity and our compass guided by our faith. We will navigate our course by God's will and our desire to serve our Captain. "Where there's a will there's a way."

As we journey through life, build and sail our ship, and encounter storms and waves of adversity, we need to rely on the instructions we've been given and use those tools of the trade to see us through. Storms come in all shapes, sizes, and intensities. An anonymous writer said, "Not all storms come to disrupt your life; some come to clear your path." The rain that falls from storms often cleans the air to make it fresh and make the sky to appear without tarnish. We are surprised at times that an adversity or trial has provided major benefits at its conclusion. Somehow we are able to find a lesson to be learned or a strength to be gained. It depends on our determination and desire, our will, and our faith.

You can find yourself observing a storm through glass windows with curiosity and wonder much like I did as a child, or you can retreat into darkness and discouragement because of fear. I don't recommend the latter. Find your faith. Explore positivity. Allow yourself to feel the raindrops gently touching your face and embrace the present. Cherish the agency that you have to make a choice. You can't always select or choose your storms, but you can choose how you will navigate through them. "Where there's a will, there's a way."

Often I find myself, now, later in my life, sitting by glass windows similar to those I sat by as a child. And during a storm, especially a thunderstorm, I casually watch the rain drizzle slowly down the glass. I notice the glass tremble and vibrate as thunder claps in the distance. My world doesn't seem as massive as it did when I was younger, but it is still my world and is adorned with blankets of memories and a garden variety of storms. I close my eyes and visualize my ship sailing over calm waters at times and enormous waves on other occasions. I can feel the cool breeze of peace gracing my face and fingering through my hair. I hear the snapping sound of the sails that ensure me that I am on course. I am able to steer my ship with oars of perseverance and have the security of an anchor that is strong and reliable, because it is founded on faith.

Although this scene can become mesmerizing, I don't escape from reality, because in reality there are always going to be storms and waves of adversity. My journey is not yet complete, and I must endure to the end. Life is a masterpiece waiting to be analyzed. I am trying life and liking it, in spite of the storms. Some storms I have gone through have definitely cleared a path for me to change course and take a different direction. And the rain that has fallen on me has made things clean and fresh around me. I had to teach myself how to dance in that rain. I have been able, through faith, to accomplish insurmountable feats. With God, nothing is impossible.

Step by step we progress. Piece by piece we become enlightened. Little by little we overcome. It doesn't happen all at once and is rarely accompanied by a miraculous event. It comes with direction from the Holy Spirit in a quiet and sacred way. God directs our course, and Jesus Christ is truly the "Captain of our souls." Our journeys are not the same and our ships are built in different ways, but we all have the same map to follow, the Plan of Salvation. Embrace who you are and what you were meant to become. Live in the present with all your being. Remember "where there's a will, there's a way." And most importantly, don't forget to dance in the rain.

END

Bibliography

Alcott, L. M. (2020, August 16). *Little Women*. Retrieved from Notable-Quotes: http://www.notable-quotes.com/a/alcott_louisa_may.html

Arkell, B. (2017, May 22). *20 Timeless Life Lessons from Gorson B. Hinckley*. Retrieved August 18, 2020, from calledtoshare.com: http:www.calledtoshare.com/2017/05/22/20-gordon-b-hinckley-quotes/

Mandela, N. (2012). *azquotes.com/qoute/185309*. Retrieved August 27, 2020, from azquotes: http://www.azquotes.com/quote/185309

Marketing, E. (2020). *Celebrate the 55th Anniversary of the Twist*. Retrieved August 17, 2020, from chubberchecker.com: http://www.chubberchecker.com

Morehead, L. (1981). *Webster Handy College Dictionary*. New York, New York: New American Library.

News, D. (2015, June). President Thomas S. Monson Greets President Boyd K. Packer. *Funeral Elder L. Tom Perry*. Retrieved August 17, 2020

Paul Vance, L. P. (1958). *Catch a Falling Star*. Retrieved August 17, 2020, from Google.com/search: http://www.google.com/search?q=catch+a+falling+star&oq=catchat&aqs=chrome.1.69.157j015j46j0.9446j0j15&sourceid=chrome&ie=UTF-8

Roosevelt, F. D. (n.d.). *topics/fear-quotes*. Retrieved August 27, 2020, from brainyquote.com: http://www.brainyquote.com/topics/fear-quotes

Saints, C. o.-D. (1853). *Zion Stands with Hills Surrounded*. Utah, USA: The Church of Jesus Christ of Latter-Day Saints. Retrieved August 18, 2020

Saints, C. o.-D. (1985). *Hymns*. Salt Lake City, Utah: The Church of Jesus Christ of Latter-Day Saints.

Saints, C. o.-D. (2004). *Preach My Gospel*. Salt Lake City, Utah, USA: Church of Jesus Christ of Latter-Day Saints. Retrieved August 27, 2020

Saints, C. o.-D. (2007). *Teachings of Presidents of the Church*. Salt Lake City, Utah, USA: The Church of Jesus Christ of Latter-Day Saints. Retrieved August 18, 2020

Schultz, C. (1950). *The Peanuts Gang*. Seattle, Washington, USA: Fantagraphics Books. Retrieved August 18, 2020

Stein, J. (1964). *Fiddler on the Roof*. Milwaukee, Wisconsin: Hal Leonard Publishing Corp. Retrieved August 17, 2020

TAylor, J. (1806). *The Star*. Retrieved August 17, 2020, from Google.com/search: hyyp://www.google.com/search?qs_ssp=eJzj4+DP1TcwL8goMmD0Yisp28zLzgEAMdUFqQ&q=twinkle&aqs=chrome.5.69i57j0l4j46j0l2.9947j0j15&sourceid=c...

www.ingramcontent.com/pod-product-compliance
Lightning Source LLC
Chambersburg PA
CBHW022024090426
42739CB00006BA/269